Get your act together, Cinderella!

Get your act together, Cinderella!

A call to the church of today

Michael Griffiths

Inter-Varsity Press
STL Books

INTER-VARSITY PRESS
38 De Montfort Street, Leicester LE1 7GP, England
STL Books, PO Box 48, Bromley, Kent, England

Unless otherwise stated, Scripture quotations in this publication are from the Holy Bible, New International Version. Copyright © 1973, 1978, 1984 International Bible Society. Published by Hodder & Stoughton.

First published 1989

British Library Cataloguing in Publication Data
Griffiths, Michael, *1928–*
Get your act together, Cinderella: a call
to the church of today.
1. Christian church
I. Title
260

IVP ISBN 0-85110-668-4
STL ISBN 1-85078-057-9

Set in Linotron Baskerville
Typeset in Great Britain by
Parker Typesetting Service, Leicester
Printed and bound in Great Britain by
Cox & Wyman Ltd, Reading

Inter-Varsity Press is the book-publishing division of the Universities and Colleges Christian Fellowship (formerly the Inter-Varsity Fellowship), a student movement linking Christian Unions in universities and colleges throughout the United Kingdom and the Republic of Ireland, and a member movement of the International Fellowship of Evangelical Students. For information about local and national activities write to UCCF, 38 De Montfort Street, Leicester LE1 7GP.

STL Books are published by Send The Light (Operation Mobilisation), PO Box 48, Bromley, Kent.

CONTENTS

Introduction for Non-Christian Readers

Today there are so many different denominational churches, and even some churches that call themselves undenominational. They all feel that the way they do things in their church is the only right way, and that other people are all wrong. This can be confusing and discouraging, making us doubt whether any of them are right. Some of the churches seem very unconvincing compared with Jesus of Nazareth, and their formality and institutionalism can be very off-putting.

Are there simple principles that will help us to understand why all these different groups exist? How can someone decide which of the many possible churches he or she ought to join?

Sometimes people who have been Christians for a long time feel very disenchanted by the church they belong to because its members seem to be so divided on various issues. Many people seem to be in congregations where there is disagreement and unhappiness, and people pulling out to go to other churches, or even starting new ones of their own. This may shake our confidence in the rightness of Christian beliefs generally. It does not seem unreasonable for non-Christians to be asking the question: 'If the Christian faith is the truth, why are Christians always being somewhat disagreeable to one another? Why is there so little agreement?'

And anyway, what is the point of 'going to church'? Can't one be a proper Christian all on one's own? Is all this singing of hymns and choruses really necessary, and what is the point of having 'services'? Would the God of the Bible really want to be 'worshipped' all the time, as some of these people seem to think?

This book attemps to answer these and many other questions.

Introduction for Christian Readers

There is no doubt that the church is the greatest hindrance to evangelizing the world! Non-Christians are attracted by the Lord Jesus: they have no problems with him. It's the Christians and the church they cannot stand! If Christians themselves are vague about the purpose of the church, it is not surprising that non-Christians find that one of the greatest stumbling blocks to faith is their inability to understand the churches or to find in them the winsomeness of Jesus in a convincing way. They complain of dullness, formality, irrelevance and boredom. This book is to help Christians (and perhaps some non-Christians too) to understand what the church is really all about.

I wanted originally to call this book *Cinderella with Ataxia* in order to make clear its relationship with my earlier book *Cinderella with Amnesia* (IVP, 1975). The idea of that title was that the bride of Christ was like Cinderella sitting in the institutional ashes, having lost her memory, having forgotten who she is and apparently not remembering that she is supposed to be getting herself ready for the coming Prince. The idea of my second title was that while Cinderella may by now have partially recovered her memory, she suffers from a lack of co-ordination of her members. (One *Oxford English Dictionary* definition of ataxia is 'inability to co-ordinate the voluntary movements'). But the publishers in their wisdom rightly suspected that even their informed readership might be excused for not knowing what 'ataxia' is! So we have devised a title which establishes a relationship with the earlier book and reminds us of the confusion, lack of co-ordination and failure in communication between the various parts of the church, the bride of Christ.

When I received the request to write a book for IVP about the doctrine of the church, I was pleased because I had been feeling in my bones for some time that I wanted to write such a book. Being a busy missionary in the Far East at the time, I felt that it was a matter of principle only to write if invited to do so, rather than submitting unsolicited manuscripts. In due course, still working in Asia, I was startled to discover how well *Cinderella with Amnesia* was being received, not only in the UK but in translation also.

Both the English and American editions are now out of print as the churches have been changing so rapidly that the material is out of date. In the intervening years there has been a great deal of thought, and many new books, about the doctrine of the church. The rather casual attitude towards the local church which characterized my own generation in the years after the war has been replaced by a much more serious and responsible attitude. This changing attitude has meant that what seemed to be startling innovative suggestions in 1975 are now thought of as commonplace (in countries like England and New Zealand, if not in more conservative areas of Wales, Scotland and Ireland).

And now IVP have suggested that I might write a completely new book for the last decade of the twentieth century, which would not only cover the basic doctrine, but also deal with various other relevant issues and problems for church life which have arisen since the earlier book was written. Let me give one obvious example: in *Cinderella with Amnesia* great

10

emphasis was laid upon corporateness, criticizing individuals who were spiritual freelances, having only the loosest of ties with a local church, perhaps justifying their individualism by saying, 'I am a member of the universal church!' Christians were to see that building the local church was a worthy goal, a satisfying lifework for every believer. It still is – and hardly anyone would disagree: such an emphasis now seems *passé*, 'trad.' and self-evident. Things have changed so far in the intervening years that some people have taken the importance of the local church to absurd lengths. They have exaggerated the authority of the congregation to the extent that the individual almost loses responsibility for making decisions of his own.

Today it seems to me that the great issue is not the local church any more, but the universal church: how do local churches relate to the universal church? Do we run our own show, and build up our own work, encourage transfer growth from other churches to our own ('we alone after all are biblical'!) and trust that it will become the largest and most 'successful' church in the area?

Once we start to think about such attitudes, and ask New Testament questions, it becomes clear that to think like this about other churches is not biblical at all. How can one care only for the growth of one congregation and not care that God should be equally glorified in all other churches that bear his name? This inward-looking doctrine of the local church is selfish – little removed from the selfish individualism that preceded it. Individual selfishness has progressed to corporate selfishness – it is the same sin on a larger corporate scale!

Thus it seems to me that Cinderella may have recovered from amnesia, and got her memory back (partially perhaps). But she is still suffering from lack of co-ordination, and the time when all the parts are working properly (Eph. 4:16) still seems a long way off!

11

This book is an entirely different book from its predecessor and its outline contents was planned without any reference to the previous book (authors forget almost as fast as readers!). Most people's thinking should have progressed over the years. At a later stage I went back to the earlier book to see if there were ideas or illustrations which should still find some place in a book intended as a general handbook on the doctrine of the church. One subject which is not included, and might seem to be an extraordinary omission, is that of spiritual gifts, and also the giving of spiritual gifts to women. The main reason for this apparent omission is that I have written on the subject in some detail in *Serving Grace: Gifts Without Inverted Commas* which was published in 1986 by MARC Europe. In this present book I have had space only to look at these matters briefly in chapter 8 which is on ministry.

The danger in writing this or any book on the doctrine of the church is that one may be merely negative. There is widespread disillusionment with the old structures, and Christians are disappointed in their own congregations. This holy disquiet must be better than either the old complacency or the new irresponsibility: we all have much higher expectations today of what we want our churches to be becoming. But it is not enough to diagnose the symptoms of the churches' maladies, there must be an attempt to prescribe treatment. We must be able to look ahead to see where we think churches ought to be going, and how they might be able to co-operate in such a way that they are co-ordinated by the Spirit.

I long that those who read this book might not merely desire a more beautiful and credible church, but throw in all their energies to build up the body of Christ until we all arrive at the unity of the faith.

Michael Griffiths

IS THIS YOUR CHURCH?
ACTS 2:44–47 – A Modern Version

[44] And all those who had believed were apart and had nothing in common; [45] and they began hoarding their possessions and property and neglecting anyone who might have need. [46] And once a week the religious met for Sunday morning worship, and twice a week the spiritual met for Sunday morning worship plus Sunday evening worship plus Wednesday night Bible study. And all assembled with a divided mind, in their own churches on their own corners. And afterwards they all retreated to their houses in suburbia, to live the rest of the week apart from each other and in a lifestyle acceptable to their pagan neighbours. And they ate alone in sadness and insecurity, [47] blaming God for their troubles. And they were laughed at by their neighbours. And God withheld from their midst any power or blessing and their number decreased day by day.

(after Grant Edwards in The Other Side, *Issue 134, November 1982)*

OR THIS?
ACTS 2:44–47 – New International Version

[44] All the believers were together and had everything in common. [45] Selling their possessions and goods, they gave to anyone as he had need. [46] Every day they continued to meet together in the temple courts. They broke bread in their homes and ate together with glad and sincere hearts, [47] praising God and enjoying the favour of all the people. And the Lord added to their number daily those who were being saved.

14

THE NATURE OF
THE CHURCH
What is it?

'The church is the teaching of Christ made visible.'
(Vinoth Ramachandra)

The church is the personalization of Christ's teaching.
His teaching is not just to be verbalized by people, but is
to be demonstrated concretely in the life of a human
community. The church is not merely the result of
Christ's doctrine, but is the visible evidence of its credibility. A Japanese friend of mine, Hisashi Ariga, was
once asked to define evangelism from the New Testament, and he concluded that 'the New Testament
method of evangelism was – the life of the Christian
community'. 'Church' is that Christian community
wherever and however it is encountered.

Jesus of Nazareth gathered around him a group of
disciples, and from them chose twelve whom he called
apostles. This group was the nucleus around which
the first New Testament 'church' in Jerusalem was
founded: as a community of disciples, seeking to imitate
their Master, to model his perfect lifestyle in a corporate
community.[1] All subsequent 'churches' must equally
centre upon Jesus as teacher and Lord. He is the authentic vine, and, as the individual branches that together
make up the congregation, we have life only as it flows
from him into us.

The church is thus not simply organizational, an aggregation of individuals who believe in Jesus, but an organism. If the Lord Jesus is both our teacher and our model, he is also the source of our life together, the power which enables us to function. Thus, he can call it 'my church' (Mt. 16:18), and Paul calls it 'the body of Christ' (Eph. 4:12).

Our concept of the church

Having said all this, we must lay some basic groundwork about the words we use. We all have a mental concept of 'church' based upon our own limited experience of one or more specific congregations. As the Ganda proverb has it: he who never visits thinks his mother is the only cook.[2] The most difficult part of the doctrine of the church is clearing away all the misconceptions and distorted mental images that we already have. If only we could wipe our memories clean and start all over again with the Bible and the Holy Spirit to interpret it to us!

In taking New Testament words we have to translate them into other existing words in our own language, which already have a flavour and meaning of their own. This is a translation problem, for unless we use some foreign word and define it from scratch (*e.g. ekklēsia*, the original Greek word used in the New Testament itself), we must use some existing word that already conveys some meaning to its hearers, even though its origin and associations may be entirely different. We may distort the biblical meaning by doing this unless we redefine it very carefully.

When Tyndale first translated the Bible into English he translated the word *ekklēsia* as 'congregation' throughout, avoiding using the word 'church' except in Acts 19:37, which he translated as 'robbers of heathen churches'. This reading was retained by the Authorized Version, but was replaced in the Revised Version by 'robbers of temples'. How different would the concept of 'church' have been in the popular mind if it had always been thought of as a *congregation* of human beings.

Unfortunately King James's translators used the word 'church' where Tyndale had used the word 'congregation', leaving most English speakers a sad legacy: the view that the 'church' is a building in which a congregation may or may not be meeting!

The English word 'church' derives from the Greek *kyriakos* meaning 'the Lord's', as in *kyriakē oikia*, 'the Lord's house'. And many other European languages use very similar derivations – kirk (Scots), *Kirche* (German), *kerk* (Dutch), *etc.*, while others, like *église* (French), *eglwys* (Welsh), and *iglesia* (Spanish), seem to have come more directly from the New Testament word *ekklēsia*.

In Japan, Korea and China the words used are *kyookai* (Japanese), *kyoohei* (Korean) and *jahwei* (Mandarin), and although the pronunciation differs all three use the same pair of Chinese characters meaning 'teaching association'. This meaning accommodates to Confucian ideas, but unfortunately suggests that the church is an adult education group being lectured in a classroom by a professional religious teacher. This translation may well have obscured the true biblical meaning and hindered church growth. As we shall see in chapter 6, the teaching function, ministering God's word to bless people, is primary; whereas people ministering to God in worship is really a response to God's grace, and therefore secondary.

This illustration from East Asia shows that the word we use must inevitably colour the way we think of 'church', and that it is far from simple to free any existing word of its confusing associations and to recalibrate our own mental concepts in conformity with Scripture.

Derivation of the biblical words
for 'church'

The New Testament word *ekklēsia* was originally an
ordinary secular word for a political gathering or summoned assembly of people. It was so used in Acts 19:32,
39, 41 of the riotous gathering of the citizens of
Ephesus, in a building the ruins of which still exist
today. It was also used by the Jews for 'the congregation
of Israel' which assembled before the Lord at the annual
feasts, and Stephen used it this way in Acts 7:38 of Israel
as 'the assembly in the desert'.

So because of these associations it also came to be used
of Christian gatherings. They might have used the word
synagōgē, if it had not already been in common use for
existing Jewish synagogues, so it is used only once of a
Christian gathering: in James 2:2, where it is translated
as 'meeting'.

It may well be that the early Christians adopted the
term 'church' as the nearest synonym to 'synagogue' that did not contain the strongly Jewish
undertones of the latter.[3]

Ekklēsia, however, could mean any kind of gathering,
and was also used of pagan religious societies. Frequently, therefore, a qualifying word describes what
kind of gathering is meant: *e.g.* 'my church' (Mt. 16:18),
'the church of God' (Acts 20:28; 1 Cor. 1:2; 10:32; 15:9;
1 Thes. 2:4; 1 Tim. 3:5, *etc.*) and 'churches of Christ'
(Rom. 16:16; Gal. 1:22). The fact that it is God's church
rather than ours has important implications, as we shall
see in chapter 2.[4]

The importance of the coming together of God's
people is shown by the frequency with which words
expressing 'coming together' (*synagō, synerchomai*

and *homothymadōn*) are used to describe the meetings of Christians; it is their actual coming together which is significant ... The thought of assembly is explicitly present, as in 1 Cor. 11:18; 14:19, 28, 35, where the expression is quite literally 'in church'.[5]

The first of these words, from which the noun 'synagogue' derives, is used in Acts 4:31; 11:26; 14:27; 15:30; 20:7, 8; 1 Corinthians 5:4. The second word occurs, for example, in 1 Corinthians 11:17, 18, 20, 33–34; 14:23, 26 and the third, often translated 'with one accord', is found in Acts 1:14; 2:46; 4:24; 5:12; Romans 15:6. Thus the most significant thing about the church is that it meets! That is why it is serious if some individuals 'give up meeting together as some are in the habit of doing' (Heb. 10:25).

The togetherness of Christian men is thus not secondary or contingent: it is integral to their life just as is their abiding in Christ.[6]

We need to see 'church', then, as a gathering of Christian people, who are expressing their sense of relatedness to one another in their common commitment as disciples of the Lord Jesus. And though corporeally he is in heaven now, yet through his Holy Spirit, he is present among us, and joins us together with one another and himself as 'his body'.

This simple concept of 'gathering' is seen in church confessional statements, such as Article XIX of the Thirty-nine Articles of the Church of England:

The visible Church of Christ is a congregation of faithful men (*i.e.* believing persons!), in which the pure Word of God is preached, and the Sacraments be duly ministered according to Christ's ordinance on all those things that of necessity are requisite to the same.

19

It is more important, however, to study carefully how the word is used in the Bible itself, for it is not used in the way in which we commonly and frequently hear the word 'church' used in English.

The Old Testament church

So far we have confined our thinking to the specifically Christian church that began when the Lord Jesus gathered around him a fellowship of disciples who regarded him as their teacher and leader. However, we have also seen that Stephen uses the word *ekklēsia* (Acts 7:38) for the 'congregation in the desert'. This reminds us that God had already acted to bring into existence 'a people' from the time of Abraham and then Moses, and that many of these words are then applied in turn to the New Testament church as well (*e.g.* 'a chosen people, a royal priesthood, a holy nation belonging to God' [1 Pet. 2:9]).

The Old Testament people of God would be summoned together by its leaders to worship God and to be instructed, but they were also a mobile column travelling to a destination, fighting off attacks from enemies and possessing a sense of purpose and destiny. The Old Testament usage gives us a mobile and dynamic view of the church as a group on the move to a destination (though they lost their way in the desert and wandered around for much of the forty years!). Lesslie Newbigin uses this image:

> The church is the pilgrim people of God. It is on the move – hastening to the ends of the earth to beseech all men to be reconciled to God, hastening to the end of time to meet its Lord who will gather all into one.[7]

While it is certainly possible to think of the New

20

Testament church as something quite new, founded by Jesus, we can also think of it as having some continuity with the Old Testament 'congregation of God'. Peter freely uses Old Testament images of the people of God to describe the church (1 Pet. 2:9–10). The people of God once consisted mainly of Jews, with a few Gentiles within their gates, while the church that Jesus founded was initially made up entirely of Jews, but later embraced more and more Gentiles until they were in the majority (which created great tensions for Jewish Christians torn between loyalty to fellow-Jews and to fellow-Christians who were not Jews). The image of the vine, for example, was originally used of Israel (Is. 5:1; Hos. 10:1, *etc.*), but Jesus is the authentic vine. The image of the flock was originally used of Israel (Is. 40:11; Ez. 34, *etc.*), and Jesus is the good shepherd, whose coming was promised. It seems clear that Stephen's use of the word is not merely an allusion (as one might call the Communist Party the 'church' of Karl Marx), but implies that there is some continuity, as well as discontinuity. Thus Paul argues in 1 Corinthians 10 that Israel's experience in the wilderness is a paradigm for the churches, that they may learn from Israel's example.

> This appropriation of the Old Testament ... imparted to the church a profound social and political self-consciousness, and furnished the new society with a past history as well as an outlook on the future ... a powerful historical element from which the church derived the sense that she was not merely an association of likeminded persons ... but an enduring social organism ... grounded in a continuum of historical experience and development.[8]

The first Jerusalem church found it very difficult to reconcile the concept of uncircumcised Gentiles being baptized and accepted as Christians (Acts 10:28; 11:2; 15:1). Proselytes to Judaism, mentioned by the Lord Jesus (Mt. 23:15), accepted circumcision and obedience to the Torah (especially the kosher food laws) and thus became virtually indistinguishable from Jews, having accepted their culture as well as their religion. At the famous Jerusalem Council meeting, after Peter, Barnabas and Paul had spoken (Acts 15:7, 12), the clincher was James's quotation of a passage from the prophet Amos (9:11–12), which spoke of 'Gentiles [or 'nations'] that bear my name', that is, Gentiles who were still identifiable as having a national identity which was *not* Jewish.[9]

None the less, this sense of continuity with the past was important, for they as yet had no New Testament Scriptures. Their Bible was the account of how God had dealt with the Jews, as the people of God, and they needed to apply that to themselves, not merely as interesting analogies, but as the revelation of the unchanging principles of God's dealings with people. Much of the argument in the epistles derives from the Old Testament, and they must be seen to be relevant.

The New Testament concept of 'church'

It is important, but not easy, to get the feel of the word 'church' in Scripture. Archbishop Donald Robinson writes that in the New Testament it mostly means a local congregation of Christians, and continues as follows:

Locality was essential to its character. The local ekklesia was not thought of as part of some world-wide ekklesia, which would have been a contradiction in terms ... while there might be as many churches as there were cities or even households, yet the New Testament recognized only one ekklesia without finding it necessary to explain the relationship between the one and the many. The one was not an amalgamation or federation of the many.[10]

The illustration used by Alan Stibbs has always been helpful.[11] We say 'Look at the moon!' whether what we see is a thin crescent or a full moon: we do not say 'Look at part of the moon'. It is 'moon' in character, when we see part or whole; indeed we never see more than one side at a time from earth. So also Christians meeting together are 'church'. We see only a small outcrop of a huge rock formation. In another book Alan Stibbs writes:

> ... when local congregations of Christians are referred to in the New Testament, they are not collectively called 'the Church'; that is they are not thought of as constituent parts of one organized earthly institution. Rather they are explicitly and surprisingly called, in the plural, 'the churches'.[12]

He also points out that Paul does not tell the Corinthians, 'The church has no such practice' but rather 'nor do the churches of God' (1 Cor. 11:16).

Thus we must assume that attempts to bring local churches together in associations or denominations are not truly 'church' so much as 'para-church' – and that the Vatican, Church House, the Baptist Union, Methodist Conference, Coastlands and the like are just as much para-church as are Greenbelt, the Scripture Union, the Navigators or the Universities and Colleges Christian Fellowship (see chapter 11).

The church universal and local

While the word 'church' has many meanings in English – a building, a congregation, a denomination, a profession embraced by clerics, or the total Christian community – in the New Testament it seems to have only a single meaning – the latter one. This, however, needs some qualification so that we may also say that it is seen in two aspects, universal and local:

1. The universal church – made up of all Christians, living and dead, irrespective of their denominational prejudices, race, nationality or social status (as used in Eph. 1:22; 3:10, 21; 5:23–32). In Scripture we see this as the glorified church before the throne, the great multitude which no-one can number from every tribe, tongue and nation.

2. The local church – with the exception of the verses from Ephesians already mentioned, nearly every other reference is to a local congregation of Christians, normally meeting regularly in the same place, and with leadership whose authority is recognized by the congregation as a whole.

This helpful distinction between the two aspects of the church can be understood alongside the suggestion mentioned above that 'church' (like 'moon' or 'carboniferous limestone') can have only one essential meaning if we accept the neat description by K. L. Schmidt that the local church may be regarded as 'the total community . . . in local circumscription'.[13] Viewed in this way it is apparent that we are really trying to grasp only one concept, rather than two.

Actually Paul speaks of churches in several different ways:

1. Regionally – the 'churches' (plural) of Galatia, Macedonia or Achaia

2. Municipally – 'the church of God which is at Corinth'

3. Personally – 'the church of the Thessalonians'

4. Locally – the church in the house of Nympha, Aquila and Priscilla, *etc.*

Exclusive doctrines of the church

Religious reformers reacting against the institutional church are often prone to reject the old and to ascribe to the new an altogether enhanced view of being the only true church, a fresh reincarnation of the Pentecost church of Acts, as it were. Thus, even the most open of Christian Brethren would speak of those 'who meet as we meet in obedience to New Testament principles' and view 'the denominations' as totally apostate churches, the 'church in ruins'. In a similar way the 'kingdom churches' belonging to the restoration movement believe that among them alone is the rule of Jesus the King restored, and kingdom authority truly practised.

In these and other breakaway groups their sincerity and desire to return to the simplicity of the New Testament, free of the traditions and accretions of the passing years, are genuine and commendable. The idea has a simplicity that appeals to all of us who are impatient of institutionalized, formal Christianity. It is their perception of others which is at fault. There is often too little sense of history, and the church is seen as a sleeping beauty which has been cast into an eighteen-hundred-year sleep until the leaders of the new group fought their gallant way through the thorns to awaken her. More seriously there is a very inadequate view of the work of the Holy Spirit: it is as though he too has been asleep, dormant and unemployed until he was somehow rediscovered a few years ago!

This cannot be right. God never ceases to be God, and his promises to the church are as certain as his promises to Israel. Paul's assurances to the Roman Christians in Romans 8 could be doubted if it were thought that the Lord had broken his word to Israel. That is why he explains in Romans 9–11 that though Israel has not kept the covenant, the Lord has remained faithful, and will finally restore Israel. Ultimately 'all Israel' (all without distinction, that is, and not all without exception) will be saved.

The assumption sometimes wrongly made is that one's own church is of divine origin, while other churches are of human origin! The truth, however (see chapters 2 and 3), is that all churches, old and new alike, must be regarded at one and the same time as both fallible, sinful human organizations and God-sustained and God-indwelt organisms.

An enriched contemporary meaning

Hans Küng has some interesting things to say about the changing forms of the church:

> The historical church cannot do without this constant renewal of its form . . . It is impossible simply to preserve the Church for all time in the original form it enjoyed as the Primitive Church. Changing times demand changing forms.[14]

It is important and helpful to recognize that contextualization is not only necessary in moving from one contemporaneous culture to another, but will also be necessary in consecutive periods in the same culture.

What is true of forms is also true of mental concepts. As new words are constantly added to our language, and meanings shift, we need to keep on changing the words we use to describe the church so that the unchanging biblical concept may be kept alive and fresh in our thinking. This is the philosophy behind modern Bible translation.

This fossilization of forms that makes the church seem to be an institution out of touch with the rapid onward changes in society has to be prevented. Buildings (ancient and draughty), dress (distinctive and quaint), language (beautiful but not contemporary), music (aesthetic but archaic) – so much of this gives the impression that Christian faith is out of date. God is not out of date, but his people so often seem to be.

In every culture and in every age we must find words that convey a more dynamic image of the church. It may be a muster, or a posse where a group is called to travel with a common purpose. A great trek or a long march may be meaningful in some countries. In the Yao tribal culture where infertility necessitates babies being bought from other tribes, given a new name and tribal clothes after being chosen by loving parents, the biblical picture of 'I, and the children God has given me' (Heb. 2:13) may provide a helpful model of the new household of God into which we have been introduced by adoption.

In the sixties, student demonstrations provided a useful model, so that writing from student unrest in Japan, David Michell wrote:

> The church of God is a body which should be demonstrating all the time – demonstrating the love of God.[15]

In 1966 Alan Ginsberg, an American author, wrote a poem called *How to Make a March/Spectacle*. This poem offered the thesis that:

> Demonstrations should lay aside their usually pugnacious quality in favour of festive dancing and a chanting parade, that would pass out balloons and flowers, candy and kisses, bread and wine to everyone along the line of march – including any cops or Hell's Angels in the vicinity. The atmosphere

should be one of gaiety and affection governed by
the intention to attract or seduce participation
from the usually impassive bystanders – or at least
to overcome their worst suspicions and hostilities.[16]

This 'love demo' may sound like past history today, but
the Watford churches did something very like it
recently to make the public aware that they were about
to start a mission. It was an attractive image for the
church and still is, although it is becoming dated and
lacks a sufficiently contemporary feel.

Perhaps royal weddings, walkabouts, and Olympic
Games processions are today's equivalents of the
Roman triumphs or Jerusalem festivals that gave a
model of festivity, rejoicing and onward movement
centred around a royal personage. Perhaps a Royal
Gala Performance with plenty of audience participation
might convey something of the right idea!

The reader is urged to pause at this point to think
about his or her mental image of the church. Can we see
it as a community of those disciples of Jesus committed
to a corporate lifestyle and motivated by the indwelling
of his Holy Spirit among us? Can we think of it not as
some vintage car, now stalled and stationary, but like a
contemporary vehicle, advertised for its ability to speed
along dangerous roads in the most dreadful weather to
its heavenly destination? This may be somewhat difficult, because though we know it is God's church and
Christ's body, its weak human frailty, so glaringly
obvious, obscures its divine origins. It is to a consideration of this paradox of the church being simultaneously God's church and man's church that we turn in
the next two chapters.

THE DIVINITY OF THE CHURCH
Whose is it?

*Don't you know that you yourselves are God's temple and that
God's Spirit lives in you? If anyone destroys God's temple,
God will destroy him; for God's temple is sacred, and you are
that temple. (1 Cor. 3:16–17)*

*If anyone wants to be contentious about this, we have no other
practice – nor do the churches of God.*

*Don't you have homes to eat and drink in? Or do you
despise the church of God and humiliate those who have
nothing? What shall I say to you? Shall I praise you for this?
Certainly not! (1 Cor. 11:16, 22)*

*The body is a unit, though it is made up of many parts; and
though all its parts are many, they form one body. So it is with
Christ. For we are all baptised by one Spirit into one body –
whether Jews or Greeks, slave or free – and we were all given
the one Spirit to drink.*

*Now the body is not made up of one part but of many. If the
foot should say, 'Because I am not a hand, I do not belong to
the body,' it would not for that reason cease to be part of the
body. And if the ear should say, 'Because I am not an eye, I do
not belong to the body,' it would not for that reason cease to be
part of the body. If the whole body were an eye, where would
the sense of hearing be? If the whole body were an ear, where
would the sense of smell be? But in fact God has arranged the*

parts of the body, every one of them, just as he wanted them to be. If they were all one part, where would the body be? As it is, there are many parts, but one body.

The eye cannot say to the hand, 'I don't need you!' And the head cannot say to the feet, 'I don't need you!' On the contrary, those parts of the body that seem to be weaker are indispensable, and the parts that we think are less honourable we treat with special honour. And the parts that are unpresentable are treated with special modesty, while our presentable parts need no special treatment. But God has combined the members of the body and has given greater honour to the parts that lacked it, so that there should be no division in the body, but that its parts should have equal concern for each other. If the one part suffers, every part suffers with it; if one part is honoured, every part rejoices with it.

Now you are the body of Christ, and each one of you is a part of it. (1 Cor. 12:12–27)

If we are keen to start a new, beautiful church then we shall probably stress the fallibility and sinfulness of other churches, while seeing our own as a unique work of God's Spirit. Yet we must recognize that all congregations are, at the same time, both the result of the work of God and a sinful, fallible human organization.

The Corinthian church is in doctrinal error over the resurrection. Some of its members are flagrant moral offenders, its meetings lack decency and order, it is divided into factions championing different leaders, some are puffed up against others; while rich people stuff themselves, others go hungry. Paul describes its members as being childish and carnal or worldly. Anyone belonging to such a church today might be tempted to despair, or more likely to look for an alternative, perhaps moving out with some likeminded brothers and sisters, to form a new, purer congregation. This seems to have been an alternative which never occurred to the first Christians, and it is their factions which Paul immediately rebukes in the opening section of 1 Corinthians.

Astonishingly, the same congregation is described as 'the temple of God' (3:16–17), 'the church of God' (11:22) and 'the body of Christ' (12:12–27). Peter, in his first letter written to scattered refugees who fled persecution in Italy to find haven in remote Asia Minor, calls the church 'the flock of God' (1 Pet. 5:2). In the next chapter we will consider the paradox of the sinfulness and frailty of local churches as fallible human organizations, but in this chapter we will explore these biblical images of the church which emphasize its divine origin. Whose church is it? Not our pastor's little kingdom, not our elders' empire, not the pope's nor our diocesan bishop's, not even ours as a human congregation, but God's!

Let's look at these several descriptions of the Corinthian church in particular (God's church, God's field, God's temple and the body of Christ), and then at some images from 1 Peter.

The church of God (1 Cor. 11:22)

In chapter 11 the Corinthian Christians are reminded that the churches of God have no other custom (11:16) and rebuke is given to those social divisions in the church which mean that some stuff themselves, while others go hungry. 'Do you despise the church of God . . .?' Paul asks them. The fact that the church belongs to God and not to man must affect our attitude towards *every Christian community*, and not just our own. If we write off other churches as 'dead', 'stuffy' or 'liberal' when God is at work among them still, then we may be 'despising' God's work.

Certainly, as we have seen, because the word *ekklēsia* has a secular and everyday meaning, it needs some qualifying description to make it clear what kind of

31

congregation is being described. But 'of God' also tells us that this church belongs to God. It is not the property of people, or some human organization like the Church Commissioners or Methodist Conference. They may have some legal rights over the buildings perhaps, but, just as in the phrases 'people of God', 'sons of God', the stress is on the church as God's own possession.

If the derivation of the word speaks of the church as being called out and summoned, there can be no doubt who has called them out and summoned them together. The opening verses of Romans refer four times to 'calling'. Chapter 4 of the letter to the Ephesians urges them to live a life worthy of the calling with which they have been called (4:1), and reminds them that they were called to one hope (4:4). It is God himself who has called the church into existence.

Consider the suggestion sometimes made today that some newly formed churches are the 'new wineskins', whereas other older, denominational churches are the 'old wineskins'. The language is biblical, but the application is not. It seems to suggest that the Lord is interested only in new churches and not in old ones. This impugns his faithfulness: it says God is fickle. It says that he is like a petulant child who soon tires of his old toys and wants new ones. Listen instead to the New Testament:

> . . . being confident of this, that he who began a good work in you will carry it on to completion until the day of Christ Jesus. (Phil. 1:6)

When God begins something, he finishes it. If the church is God's church then he will certainly bring it to completion.

The plantation of God (1 Cor. 3:9)

In 1 Corinthians 3 the Christians are shown to be childish and carnal, and the apostles who plant and water are shown to be just servants of God who gives the growth. 'You (Corinthian Christians) are God's field; you are God's building' (3:9). The stress of the original word order is 'God's fellow workers you are; God's field you are; God's building you are'. The Greek word is used only here in the New Testament and may be translated as 'field' or 'plantation'. The words translated 'field' and 'building' refer not just to the area of ground or materials of the building, but to the whole process of farming and the total project of building. It tells us that God has a great purpose, that he intends a crop and a harvest, and needs workers for his project. The images of harvestfield and vineyard are widely used in the gospels. The owner is the Lord himself. The parable of the vineyard (Mt. 21:28–41; Mk. 12:1–9; Lk. 20:9–16) speaks of the Lord as the landowner, whose tenants are trying to take over what is rightly his.

It is helpful to remember that however much we may be hurt, however zealous for the church, and however resentful of its inconsistencies and corruptions, its present leaders are only tenants in God's own project. I recently heard of a Baptist church whose leaders persuaded its members of what seemed spiritual principles of leadership, that each person should be answerable to others who would 'shepherd' them. The leaders of the church also accepted the 'shepherding' of strong spiritual personalities outside it. Yet in doing this the traditional Baptist principle of congregational government had been lost. Without realizing it they had allowed others to usurp the leadership of their congregation, people who were not even members of it! They had thrown away their birthright of congregational independence – and were no longer Baptists in the original meaning of that word. This take-over bid had been done with the highest spiritual motives, and the church became built into what is doubtless intended to be a spiritual organization. It is easy to forget that churches belong to the Lord; they are his field and are not to be taken over by tenants, no matter how sincere and genuine they are as believers.

The temple of God
(1 Cor. 3:16–17; 1 Pet. 2:4–5)

The church is more than an association of human beings with common interests. It is true that God does not dwell in temples made by human hands (Acts 7:48; 17:24) and that heaven is his throne and earth his footstool, so great is he. But he is also pleased to live within the temple made of living stones (1 Pet. 2:4–5). The visitor may recognize that 'God is really among you' (1 Cor. 14:25), and this is exactly what God has promised to those who love and obey: 'we will come to him and make our home with him' (Jn. 14:23). God himself is present in a special sense when his people come together (Mt. 18:20).

1 Corinthians 3:16–17 continues the earlier analogy (verses 9–15) of God's building project, in which Paul has laid the foundation and Cephas and others have laid further courses of bricks. Paul calls himself the master-builder (verse 3), and warns of the dangers of shoddy workmanship by human builders. But it is God's project carried out by God's servants, who will be judged on the quality of their work. There follows the strongest warning against those who engage in demolition – that those who destroy 'the temple of God', God will in turn destroy!

There are well-meaning, sincere Christians today who are deeply concerned about the sinfulness,

34

shallowness and hypocrisy of some churches, and who are tempted to divide congregations, to pull out to form some new, purer congregation of their own. They are irresponsible (albeit well-meaning) if they destroy an existing congregation in order to start their own new one. The process is not given any quasi-biblical sanction by calling the existing church an 'old wineskin'. But our polemics and despising of the church of God are not justified by using biblical vocabulary out of context: we may be guilty of destroying the temple of God, and must face the possibility that God will therefore destroy us. It is remarkable how often those who divide off to form a new church soon suffer another division, when others divide off from them in turn.

Let's unpack this analogy of the congregation as a living temple. Peter also uses it in his epistle, describing us as 'living stones' who are being built into a spiritual house (i.e. temple), resting upon the living and precious cornerstone of Jesus Christ. The implication is that this temple is still being completed, just as many cathedrals took centuries to build. There is good, responsible building with gold, silver and precious stone, but there is also building with what proves to be weak, combustible material. We are not then to think of the church as a finished masterpiece, beautiful in all its proportions. It is much more like a structure still under construction, with scaffolding around it, and with an unfinished look to it. Though it is God's temple already, the context makes it clear that human builders will be held responsible for the quality of their work. We must accept responsibility for the present state of the church, and seek by God's grace to develop it from a construction site into a beautiful, durable and lasting building.

The body of Christ (1 Cor. 12:27)

'Body' is by far the commonest word used to describe the church in terms of the number of occurrences and verses in which it is found (more than 30, including 17 in 1 Corinthians 12, 7 in Ephesians, 5 in Colossians and 2 in Romans 12: 4–5).

Unlike most of the other metaphors, the 'body of Christ' has no convincing derivation from the Old Testament, unless it is the hipbones, thighbones, *etc.*, of Ezekiel's vision (Ezk. 37). It seems possible that Paul gained some of his understanding from his 'beloved physician' Dr Luke, and he uses some of the Greek Galen's medical terminology. For instance, the equipping (Eph. 4:12) of the saints is a technical term for the 'reduction' of dislocations and fractures, so that it has some bearing on the 'ataxia' notion also, and is used by the apostle in a body context.

There is another possible interesting source for this metaphor.

Paul would often have wandered around Corinth and seen the votive offerings outside the temple of Aesclepius, the Greek god of healing. A collection of these can be found in the Corinth Museum. These terracotta models, or casts, of arms, legs, breasts and unpresentable, weaker parts (1 Cor. 12:23) may well have suggested to the apostle the fact that parts of the body need each other.[1]

How figurative is this metaphor? We assume it is easy to separate the figurative and non-figurative uses of words. Sometimes a figurative word like *ekklēsia* becomes entirely literal in meaning, or a word like 'slave', that originally meant a literal bondman, becomes an image for commitment to Christ. Often words have both literal and figurative meanings, and it becomes difficult to know whether one or the other, or both, is intended. Paul Minear in his book[2] writes:

36

Images . . . often serve a quite different function, that is, as a mode for perceiving a given reality, especially where this reality is not amenable to objective visibility or measurement.[3]

The image of the body may be used to illustrate many different emphases:

1. The solidarity and common experience of the body – to correct individualism.
2. The variety of different functions in a body – to correct overvaluation or undervaluation of one gift.
3. The co-operative and complementary functions of the body – to correct those who covet prominent gifts.
4. The necessity of the members belonging to a body – to correct those who think they don't need others.
5. Some 'unpresentable' parts have crucial functions to perform – to correct those who think others don't need them.
6. It does not exist for itself, it is the body 'of Christ' – to correct those who fail to put Christ first.

An important question is whether the 'body of Christ' applies to the local church or the church universal? Clearly in Corinthians and Romans the local congregation would have relatively few members who might be described as arms, legs, eyes and ears. While Robert Brow tried to apply the image to the world church,[4] any illustration based on being an individual cell or molecule would be an anachronism. The analogy of blood cells is very pleasing perhaps, but Paul had no microscope – and who wants to be a cell in the gluteus muscle of the church dormant! If our earlier discussion of the nature of the church is correct, then it is the local church which is mainly in mind even in Ephesians and Colossians.

How far can we take the analogy? Certainly it means much more than the body of Christians, like any corporate or collegiate body. It is the body of Christ, that which belongs to Christ, so that the 'of' is a possessive genitive, and also an objective genitive. But it is more: the body which is organically related to Christ, joined to Christ by faith and animated by the power of His Spirit. Some go further and speak of the body which may be identified with Christ, so that the 'of' is a subjective genitive. They are saying that Christ is still incarnate on earth in the church. Thus what has been figurative is thought of as literal.

In my view, while I accept the first three of these meanings, I feel that the fourth is pressing a helpful analogy too far: it obscures the fact of the ascended Christ in heaven, whose human body is in heaven; it overstresses the divine nature of the church and ignores its sinfulness, fallibility, stupidity and humanness. And assuming that this is a visible church, there is serious danger of identifying it with a denomination, such as the Roman Church, the Anglican or Lutheran Church. This 'incarnation ecclesiology' then speaks of church disunity as the rending apart of the body of Christ, an application which the New Testament never makes (though it does talk of destroying the temple of God). As Cranmer and others denied the corporeal presence of Christ on earth in opposing false sacramentalism, so we should deny his incarnate presence on earth in face of a false ecclesiasticism.[5] The 'body' is an illustration, a helpful metaphor, but it must not be pressed to absurd lengths: how can a sinful body of fallible human beings be identified with the risen Christ?[6]

The people of God (1 Pet. 2:9–10)

It is clear from the way Peter is conflating two Old Testament passages about Israel (Ex. 19:6 and Is.

38

43:20) that he is taking language used originally of the Jewish nation and applying it now to the Christian church. He adds a further reference to Hosea 2:23 where those who were not a people have now been made the people of God. They are the chosen people, the elect of God.

The church is God's elect, God's chosen people, not 'my little gang'. As a small boy I used to imagine my own fantasy gang, made up of all the nicest boys (and girls) that I knew, and we would have all manner of adventures as I dropped off to sleep. But the church is chosen by God, and he still chooses as mixed-up a group of mixed-up people as the motley crew the Lord Jesus first summoned together. We must accept those whom he chooses and calls: we cannot discriminate against, excommunicate or even cold-shoulder those whose faces or opinions we do not approve of (I am not here talking about church discipline of heresy or unrepented sin, of course). They may not be the people we would have chosen. When I served as General Director of a large mission with a distinguished history, I would have liked all our missionaries to have been 'brave warriors, their faces . . . the faces of lions . . . swift as gazelles in the mountains' (1 Ch. 12:8)! In reality, there were not so many outwardly mighty or wise. But the Lord does not look on the outward appearance and I had to accept that he was doing the choosing, and that it was his chosen group rather than mine.

The idea of the invisible church, in its popular use, derives its main attraction . . . from the fact that each of us can determine its membership as he will. It is *our* ideal church, containing the people whom we – in our present stage of spiritual development – would regard as fit members. . . . The congregation of God is something quite different. It is the company of people whom it has pleased God to call. . . . Its member are chosen by him, not by us, and we have to accept them whether we like them or not. It is not a segregation but a congregation . . . [7]

I cannot actually or mentally excommunicate those whom God himself has called and chosen to be his own. They are God's chosen people.

The flock of God (1 Pet. 5:2)

This metaphor has rich Old Testament background in Psalm 23; Isaiah 40 and supremely in Ezekiel 34 where the shepherds (*i.e.* kings and leaders) of Israel have failed, and where the Lord himself promises to come and shepherd his flock (in context, the southern kingdom of Judah). In the New Testament Jesus presents himself as the 'Good Shepherd' prophesied by Ezekiel (Jn. 10) and the shepherd who looks for lost sheep (Lk. 15). After the resurrection at the breakfast picnic by the lake, Jesus tells Peter to look after his sheep and lambs (Jn. 21:15–17), and it is this image which Peter, not surprisingly, picks up when he reminds us that the Chief Shepherd will appear, but that meanwhile the elders are called to 'shepherd' the flock of God (1 Pet. 5:2–4). They are to oversee it, as shepherds stood on some knoll overlooking the flock, a point of vantage from which they could see sheep wandering off, or wolves attacking.

But the flock is not the elders' property: it is God's flock. Those of us who are church leaders must not make the serious mistake of treating a congregation as though they really were mindless sheep! We can press the distinction of the pastor and his flock in an unbiblical way. Even the apostles are sometimes referred to as sheep by the Lord: 'Fear not, little flock' (Lk. 12:32); the 'sheep of the flock will be scattered' (Mt. 26:31). It takes another sheep to be an 'example to the flock' – otherwise we get the farcical picture of sheep walking on their hind legs carrying a crook! Biblical images are to be used in the way in which they are used in the Bible. If you take them to extremes you will only produce absurdities. It is perhaps worth commenting to pastors who want to change everything at once that sheep can be persuaded to move together as a flock at a brisk optimum pace, but if you try to get them to gallop, they scatter off in all directions!

Conclusion

The fact that the local church is a divine institution, someone else's property, has significant consequences for our attitude towards it, whether we are members or leaders – especially if we are leaders. We cannot lightly despise it, secede from it, divide it or destroy it: those who do so, God will judge.

But there are also implications for the way in which we regard local churches other than our own, especially if they are not of our own group or tradition. Can they also be seen as God's own property, his special possession? If so, then we cannot speak derisively about them, as though God were in some way absent from them. Presumably it was by his grace and the working of his Spirit that they came into existence in the first place. He was not away from the scene until we arrived and called him back again! Surely the first apostles knew God's Spirit, no matter what happened to the medieval papacy. Surely Luther and Calvin knew the touch of God's Spirit bringing them to Reformation. So also did those makers of our British religious freedom, who shed their blood for their Protestant convictions – Cranmer, Latimer, Ridley, and others – no matter how badly the Church of England is portrayed in some Victorian novels, such as those by

Anthony Trollope. So also was the hand of God on John Wesley and the early Methodists, even though Methodism today (like all denominations) has members and congregations which seem to know little of Wesley's experience when his heart was 'strangely warmed'.

We cannot deny that God raised these churches up: but we know that churches can apostasize, grow cold and die, that sadly we may write 'Ichabod' (1 Sa. 4:21–22) over some because the glory seems to have departed from them. But equally we must affirm that the Lord who may withdraw his glory, may also be pleased to restore it again, as he very soon did with the captured ark (1 Sa. 5–6) and with the glory that Ezekiel saw both departing from Jerusalem (Ez. 10:18ff.; 11:23) and returning to it again (Ezk. 43:1–5). We cannot make the claim, either biblically or intelligently, that the Holy Spirit is with us, and not with others. Yes, the fallibility, sinfulness and stupidity of the human leaders of some churches may seem to be so manifest that the glory of God, and his sovereign power to fulfil his purposes, may seem veiled and cast into shadow. But we must hold to the faithfulness and integrity of God himself in finally achieving what he has set out to do, in spite of all the hindrances, resistance and interference run by sinful people.

The church is God's church: and when he works, who can stop him?

THE HUMANITY OF THE CHURCH
Why is it in such a mess?

Christ loved the church and gave himself up for her to make her holy, cleansing her by the washing with water through the word, and to present her to himself as a radiant church, without stain or wrinkle or any other blemish, but holy and blameless. (Eph. 5:25–27)

Brothers, I could not address you as spiritual but as worldly — mere infants in Christ. I gave you milk, not solid food; for you were not yet ready for it. Indeed you are still not ready. You are still worldly. For since there is jealousy and quarrelling among you, are you not worldly? Are you not acting like mere men? For when one says, 'I follow Paul,' and another, 'I follow Apollos,' are you not mere men?

What, after all, is Apollos? And what is Paul? Only servants, through whom you came to believe — as the Lord has assigned each to his task. I planted the seed, Apollos watered it, but God made it grow. So neither he who plants nor he who waters is anything, but only God who makes things grow. The man who plants and the man who waters have one purpose, and each will be rewarded according to his own labour. For we are God's fellow workers: you are God's field, God's building.

By the grace God has given me, I laid a foundation as an expert builder, and someone else is building on it. But each one should be careful how he builds. For no-one can lay any foundation other than the one already laid, which is Jesus Christ. If any man builds on this foundation using gold, silver, costly stones, wood, hay or straw, his work will be shown for what it is, because the Day will bring it to light. It will be revealed with fire, and the fire will test the quality of each man's work. If what he has built survives, he will receive his reward. If it is burned up, he will suffer loss; he himself will be saved but only as one escaping through the flames.

Don't you know that you yourselves are God's temple and that God's Spirit lives in you? If anyone destroys God's temple, God will destroy him; for God's temple is sacred, and you are that temple. (1 Cor. 3:1–17)

We know that the Lord Jesus is both divine and human. We much less commonly speak of the church in this way. One notes with some amusement that modernist radicals who often question the divinity of Christ seem to be far more ready to insist on the divine nature of the church! Assemblies of Christians may believe that the congregation is 'God's temple' (1 Cor. 3:16) but fail to see that the same church is also childish and carnal (1 Cor. 3:3). This failure to appreciate that Scripture teaches both truths causes deep problems.

Some, however, like Bishop Newbigin of the Church of South India, see this truth very clearly:

No honest person can deny that the church as a visible institution has in the course of its history, been guilty of pride, greed, sloth and culpable blindness. Nor can we admit the possiblity of easing the difficulty by making a radical distinction between the church and its members. The 'individual Christian' is such only as a member of Christ and there can be no meaning in saying that the body of Christ cannot sin but his members can. Nor, finally, does the New Testament leave us in doubt that the church *does* sin. The words, 'Ye are the body of Christ' and the words, 'Ye are yet carnal', were addressed by the same apostle to the same body of men and women.[1]

Hans Küng, a Roman Catholic theologian, in his book *The Church*, includes a very moving section called 'Sinful and yet holy'. Küng draws the conclusion that 'the Church is a sinful church', saying that many romantic and idealistic descriptions of the 'nature' of the church bear little relations to its 'actual form'. There has been re-formation, but there has also been de-formation. He says:

> The history of the Church is not only a very human history, but a deeply sinful history, and it has always been so. We have only to read the New Testament epistles to be confronted with the sad reality of sin.[2]

On the one hand the church is the body of Christ, and he is pleased to dwell among us: just as his Holy Spirit is willing to live in the heart of the individual Christian believer, though he is still a sinner. On the other hand, the church is a *fallible, sinful, human* organization, just as much as the Christian believer is still a sinful human being. I find this is a very liberating truth. Just as we make allowances for our own humanness, and that of others, so also we need to make allowances for the fact that the local church is made up of sinful, fallible men and women. Some of our leaders can sometimes be stupid, silly, pompous, and self-seeking as well as fallible and sinful.

Many of our problems arise because we confuse the glory of the Lord indwelling his church (*e.g.* 2 Cor. 6:16), with the very human nature of it. Among the Christian Brethren the traditional emphasis at the breaking of bread service is on justification and the perfection of the believer by virtue of justification, through the blood and merits of our Lord Jesus Christ. We praise God for perfecting us in Christ. Hallelujah! But in so doing we ignore the imperfect progress of our sanctification. I was once publicly rebuked at the Lord's table for announcing a hymn of Wesley's which includes the line, 'Foul, I to the fountain fly'. This was in an assembly which had earlier had a major row over another hymn, which ran 'He brings a poor vile sinner into his house of wine'. This hymn was also banned as inappropriate to the Lord's table where we meet as perfected saints, justified in Christ. It was an over-emphasis on our being 'God's temple' without remembering that we are also very human and 'yet carnal'.

1. The primitive church was not perfect

The lack of perfection in the primitive church is not self-evident. All biblical reforming movements take the church of the New Testament as a model. 'We follow New Testament principles', we boast. Some wings of the 'renewal' and 'restoration' movements make this assumption that we are restoring primitive perfection. We see them as 'Spirit-filled' and therefore perfect; or pure in their simplicity and lack of institutionalism. We certainly should take them as our model for today, but not as a perfect, ideal, impeccable church, which cannot make mistakes and need not make any progress. Many of us, including myself, do find 'primitivism' has a real appeal, especially when we are feeling very disen-chanted with our churches. 'Let's scrap everything and go back to the beginning' seems a better alternative: but you cannot just ignore history like that.

This is an important point, so let me develop it systematically by looking at the gospels, Acts, the epistles, and Revelation.

a. The gospels

The apostolic band is seen as a group of sinful, quarrelling, competing men. They are concerned for their own prestige – which of them is the greatest (Lk. 9:46; 22:24). They seem, repeatedly, to be out of sympathy with the Lord Jesus, and he grieves over their lack of understanding. James and John, as one might expect of two nicknamed Sons of Thunder, want the Lord to bring down fire from heaven upon a Samaritan village, in imitation of Elijah (Lk. 9:54ff.). After the resurrection they are still asking questions like 'Lord, are you at this time going to restore the kingdom to Israel?' (Acts 1:6). There is no evidence that the twelve apostles chosen by the Lord are perfect in their understanding of truth, their sympathy with their Lord or their Christian profession. One was Judas who betrayed him, and another Peter, who denied him three times.

It seems naïve to assume that they were totally and instantaneously transformed by the Pentecost experience, as though indwelling by the Spirit, or baptism in the Spirit, completely changed them in every respect. Certainly we are told of a new boldness which they had prayed for (Acts 4:13, 29, 31), but as we shall see they were neither impeccable nor infallible.

b. The Acts

It seems simplest to list evidence of the fallibility of the early Christians, not because we are any better, but to recognize the plain facts.

The hypocrisy and deceit of Ananias and Sapphira (5:1–11)
The 'complaining' between different ethnic groups (6:1–7)
Love of limelight and wrong motivation in Simon Magus (8:9–24)
The circumcized believers 'criticized' Peter (11:1–2)

47

Unbelief that their prayers for Peter had been heard (12:15)
The 'dispute and division' in Antioch (15:1–2)
The 'sharp disagreement' between Paul and Barnabas (15:39)

It just is not correct to regard the early church as being a perfect church. Yes, it knew the work of the Holy Spirit and it was committed and ready to suffer in a most remarkable way: but it was still sinful and fallible. In spite of Acts 1:8 it was incredibly slow to move out of the city of Jerusalem until forced out by persecution, and even slower to break free from the ties of temple-based religion. Their deep-seated racialism and nationalism made them cautious about accepting Samaritans and most reluctant to accept uncircumcised Gentiles.

c. The epistles

Had the New Testament church been perfect, it would not have been necessary to write letters to correct them. The existence of the epistles is in itself clear evidence of the fallibility and sinfulness of the churches to whom they were written. Without labouring this point let us look at the church of Corinth.

It was divided up into factions (1 Cor. 1:10ff.)
It was worldly and childish (1 Cor. 3:1ff.)
It was immoral and sinful (1 Cor. 5:1–7)
They were stumbling-blocks for one another (1 Cor. 8:9–13)
There was disorder at communion (1 Cor. 11:20f.)
They were in doctrinal error (1 Cor. 15:12f.)

The constant warnings against immorality all imply that this was a continuing problem. The warnings against disunity and divisiveness show that this too was endemic. The doctrinal sections in Galatians and

Colossians show that there was a great deal of error in the primitive churches.

The requirements of those to be appointed elders and deacons in the Pastoral Epistles show that financial greed, fondness for the bottle (among men *and* women), and pugnacious aggressiveness were common among possible candidates. Men are to pray lifting up holy hands 'without anger or disputing' (1 Tim. 2:8). There is no suggestion that the standards of behaviour in the churches was necessarily high.

d. The Revelation

The messages to the seven churches of Revelation 2–3 provide ample evidence of the frailty of the churches of Asia Minor. These are a fruitful source of prophetic preaching, because we find in them so many failures that are found equally in the churches of today.

The church of Ephesus

They have uncovered false prophets (2:2)
They have lost their first love (2:4)
They must repent (2:5)

The church of Pergamum

There is idolatry-related immorality (2:14)
There is false teaching (2:15)
They must repent (2:16)

The church of Thyatira

There is false prophecy (2:20)
They tolerate sexual immorality (2:20)
They have dabbled in the occult (2:24)

The church of Sardis

They are spiritually dead (3:1)
They are spiritually asleep (3:13)
They must repent and obey (3:3)

The church of Laodicea

They are spiritually lukewarm (3:16)
They are self-satisfied (3:17)
They must repent (3:19)

How often today do we hear churches called upon to repent?

e. Subsequent church history

> As the Church of Jerusalem, Alexandria and Antioch, have erred; so also the Church of Rome hath erred, not only in their living and manner of Ceremonies, but also in matters of Faith.[3]

We could add many other churches to the list also. In our own day there are many who want to go to wild extremes, who want immediate proofs of God's existence by healing, signs and wonders. They want to walk by sight, not by faith. The effect of culture upon Christianity injects many human traditions. The churches of the Caribbean think it sinful for women not to wear hats in church, while the churches of Greece think it sinful for women to wear trousers anywhere. In the churches of Borneo, losing your temper is seen as being as serious a sin as adultery. In the churches of China they would agree with the Borneo Christians, but few women would wear hats and nearly all would wear trousers.

One of the problems of the 'humanness' of the church is its chronic failure to respond to its pastors and teachers, and to take notice of what is preached to it. Motivating Christians in what is a 'society of consent' is difficult. Recently two young men came to me for advice because their house church required them to sign a covenant promising to submit to guidance from their elders, to give a proportion of their income regularly to the church, and not to take holidays without first consulting the church! One sensed the frustration of leaders trying hard to find ways of making Christians obey the teaching given from the pulpit. It is an old and universal problem. The Roman Catholic Church uses the confessional, and the Methodist class-meeting got members to ask one another how they had been tempted in the past week and how they had responded.

2. The primitive church sought to reform itself

The problem with an unreal and idealistic view of the church is that we fail to face up to its problems and fail to correct them as the apostles did. Consider the following examples.

a. Paul was realistic about the Cretans, even in the churches. He did not say that they were 'saints' and therefore perfect.

Even one of their own prophets has said, 'Cretans are always liars, evil brutes, lazy gluttons.' This testimony is true (Tit. 1:12).

b. The Jerusalem church reacted to racial tensions between its members: it was said that the Hellenistic widows were being neglected. So they appointed seven Hellenistic men to take charge (Acts 6:1–6).

c. A tragic separation took place between Jew and Gentile in Antioch over eating 'kosher', with both Peter and Barnabas on the wrong side. Paul did not hesitate to confront Peter to the face about it (Gal. 2:11–14).

d. Priscilla and Aquila realized that Apollos, for all his gifts, was incompletely instructed. They befriended him and helped him to get right (Acts 18:24–26).

e. When there were tensions over circumcision and food laws between Jewish and Gentile Christians, Paul organized substantial financial help from the Gentile churches to the Jewish church in Jerusalem (2 Cor. 9:1ff.).

f. The epistles were a response to the churches' imperfections. Something had to be done to deal with the errors and failings of the churches.

g. Where there were factions and disunity there were strong words to help deal with them (Eph. 4:3; Phil. 2:1–4)

h. Where there was unprofitable wrangling over words, it had to be stopped (1 Tim. 6:4ff.; 2 Tim. 2:14–18, 23f.).

3. Protestants recognized the need for continuous reformation

The Puritans recognized that 'reformation' was not something already successfully accomplished and so past and finished with. They spoke of the need for 'continuous reformation according to the Word of God'. There could be no standing still: as the Lord revealed error in the church, it had to be repented of, and the church altered.

The Brethren with their dislike of 'structure' have tended to deny the humanity of the church, holding the view that no 'organization' is needed: the Holy Spirit will guide. This is a failure to recognize that we are bound to have some form, some structure – and that while this is temporary it can be changed, reformed and improved. There is always some relation to contemporary culture, an unconscious assimilation of cultural ways of doing things.

Normal human processes are not suspended in Christians. The principles of group dynamics continue to apply to our meetings just as they do to those of unbelievers. When I was working as a church-planting missionary in Japan I experienced the changes in the new church group when the numbers began to increase, although I did not realize why that happened. The Lord does not overrule natural laws. So we recognize our humanness in the way we relate together in the group.

A call for realism

We must be realistic: the church is a fallible, sinful society made up of fallen, though redeemed, men and women. If we fail to recognize this truth, we shall be constantly disappointed and our faith will be shaken by the failures of the church, and the narrowness and foolishness of its human leaders. In the Old Testament we recognize that all human leaders have feet of clay. David, though a man after God's own heart, is a moral failure, and is unable to make clear decisions about his successor. Gideon and Saul have their triumphs, but also their failures. Solomon is a great organizational leader, but his private life is a scandal and he loses the hearts of the people. In both Old and New Testaments, godly individuals are critical of the people of God, and disappointed by their failures and their inconsistency. It is right that we too should be troubled – 'angry young men' (and women), if you like, just as the prophets of the Old Testament were. The church one day will be 'without stain or wrinkle or any other blemish' (Eph. 5:27), but that day has not yet come. Thus we shall often be disturbed, troubled and grieved by the failures of the church, just as we are over our own sins. But this will not shake our faith, or tempt us to walk out: it is only to be expected in a sinful, fallible, human organization. But the Lord has promised that not only is he working in his church now, but that one day he will perfect and finish his work.

We must fight against the deformation of the church and work constantly for its reformation: God has made us responsible for this. 'Continue to work out your salvation with fear and trembling, for it is God who works in you to will and to act according to his good purpose' (Phil. 2:12–13).

4. The church's continuing responsibility to reform, trusting in God

Scripture makes it clear that the church must accept responsibility to reform and change itself – it is not to wait passively for the Lord in his sovereignty to change and transform it, either slowly and progressively, or rapidly and remarkably in revival. Where revival is concerned we have a duty to pray for it, that the Lord will be pleased to quicken us.

But many scriptures also place upon the church the responsibility to repent, to obey, to change, to be transformed and so on. What in church-growth language might be called 'qualitative growth', could equally well be called 'continuous reformation according to the Word of God'. We could even choose to call it 'renewal'! Indeed, our churches might make more progress if we did not think of ourselves as being righteous and sufficiently reformed or renewed already, but always eager for more obedience.

Whose responsibility

Sometimes we talk as though God is responsible, and at other times as though everything depended upon us. In fact we are made responsible by God, but he works in us to will and to do. Hans Küng stresses our human responsibility:

> Renewal of form implies change of form by means of human decision and responsibility. God does not present us with the nature of the Church as an objective fact, nor does He overwhelm it with mystic inevitability, nor work in it by organic development ; he calls us

54

constantly to new decisions of faith, to a free responsibility.[4]

When Paul writes to the Romans, he commands them, 'Do not conform any longer to the pattern of this world, but be transformed by the renewing of your minds.' It is our responsibility to exercise our own wills in obeying by refusing to conform, and yet it is implied in Scripture that we are to allow God to do the transforming (Rom. 12:2). Writing to the Corinthians, Paul says, 'And we ... all ... are being transformed into his likeness ... which comes from the Lord, who is the Spirit' (2 Cor. 3:18). Again it is God who is the agent, the one who transforms us.

If the church is to become beautiful (and God is concerned that we *do* become beautiful), then we must long for it and pray for it. We cannot rest content with being sinful, fallible and human. We must pray to become what God intends, *to run towards our destiny*. We must respond to the purpose of God, desire it, embrace it and make it our own. Our greatest problem is the stationary church, satisfied with the *status quo*, which sees no need for repentance, reform, change and progress. God grant we may be delivered from remaining the ugly church and so become the beautiful church.

If the churches are to become better integrated, and our ataxia is to give way to greater co-ordination, we need to recognize the humanity and frailty of the churches, their leaders and members. This is not a negative attitude, but one that will prevent us from panicking when things go wrong and we meet difficulties. We will not be tempted to pull out, either, because we accept that the church is still sinful and imperfect.

THE UNITY OF THE CHURCH

How does it relate to other churches?

As a prisoner for the Lord, then, I urge you to live a life worthy of the calling you have received. Be completely humble and gentle; be patient, bearing with one another in love. Make every effort to keep the unity of the Spirit through the bond of peace. There is one body and one Spirit — just as you were called to one hope when you were called — one Lord, one faith, one baptism; one God and Father of all, who is over all and through all and in all.

But to each one of us grace has been given as Christ apportioned it. This is why it says:

> *'When he ascended on high,*
> *he led captives in his train*
> *and gave gifts to men.'*

(What does 'he ascended' mean except that he also descended to the lower, earthly regions? He who descended is the very one who ascended higher than all the heavens, in order to fill the whole universe.) It was he who gave some to be apostles, some to be prophets, some to be evangelists, and some to be pastors and teachers, to prepare God's people for works of service, so that the body of Christ may be built up until we all reach unity in the faith and in the knowledge of the Son of God and become mature, attaining to the whole measure of the fulness of Christ.

Then we will no longer be infants, tossed back and forth by the waves, and blown here and there by every wind of teaching and by the cunning and craftiness of men in their deceitful scheming. Instead, speaking the truth in love, we will in all things grow up into him who is the Head, that is, Christ. From him the whole body, joined and held together by every supporting ligament, grows and builds itself up in love, as each part does its work. (Eph. 4:1–16)

The two occurrences of the word unity (*henotēs*) in the New Testament are found in this passage in Ephesians. There is a present 'unity of the Spirit' which we have a responsibility for maintaining, and also a future 'unity of the faith' as a goal towards which we are moving. The passage as a whole, especially verses 4–6, speaks of the unity of the church (one body), related to the one Holy Spirit and our common calling to one and the same hope. This is related to the one Lord Jesus Christ, the one faith in him and baptism in his name, and the one God and Father to whom all true Christians must relate. The logic is inescapable.

Now this truth is especially necessary, not only because of the long-standing divisions in Christendom, but because in recent years there has been, in general, a fresh appreciation of the significance of the 'local church' after long neglect. But this truth is being emphasized now to the neglect of the doctrine of the one universal church. How, after all, are local churches to relate to one another (particularly within a limited area such as a village or city or town) within the universal church? Is it really glorifying to the Lord, to whom all these churches belong, that each should paddle its own canoe and ignore other congregations of the Lord's people, merely because they organize their canoes in a different way? Those of us in Brethren, separatist or restoration congregations need to ask ourselves this question – are these other groups to be regarded as 'churches' or not? Are they not also part of the universal body of Christ?

The unity of the church is not merely pragmatically useful. It is not just that 'it is good and pleasant when brothers live together in unity' (Ps. 133:1). Joseph says those very ironical words to his brothers: 'See that you do not fall out by the way!' (Gn. 45:24). For example, in Italy it is a constant gibe of Roman Catholic polemics that Protestants are so hopelessly divided. It would be pragmatically useful then if all Italian Protestant believers came together. But that would be an argument from expediency. This passage makes it clear that there are profound doctrinal and theological reasons why unity is important, relating to the oneness of God himself, and to his one ultimate purpose and destiny for all of his redeemed people.

1. The church is expected to enjoy the unity of the Spirit now in the present

The unity of the Spirit already exists. 'Make every effort to maintain *the unity of the Spirit* in the bond of peace.' The reference to the unity of the Spirit is almost certainly a backward allusion to the earlier reference in the letter (Eph. 2:22) where we are told that 'in him you too are being built together by his Spirit to become a dwelling in which God lives'. It is precisely because it is the Spirit's work to build us together, that we are urged to take responsibility for maintaining that unity. This great theme of the unity of the church is stated over and over again in Ephesians:

> For he himself is our peace, who has made the two *one* and has destroyed the barrier, the dividing wall . . . . His purpose was to create in himself *one*

59

new man out of the two ... and in this *one* body to reconcile both of them to God through the cross ... (Eph. 2:14–16).

This mystery is that through the gospel the Gentiles are heirs together with Israel (literally, same inheritance, same body, same membership – three compounds each prefixed with *syn*-) (Eph. 3:6).

But though this unity of the Spirit already exists, it is a frail unity which can be easily destroyed. Thus in Ephesians 4:2 we are told of the qualities which are required: 'Be completely humble and gentle; be patient, bearing with one another in love.' It is clear that 'maintaining the unity of the Spirit' is not easy and will require 'every effort' on our part in the realities of daily church life.

It is significant that it is called the 'unity of the Spirit', not only because it is the Holy Spirit's work to build us and bind us together, but because the 'fruit of the Spirit' (Gal. 5:22) is needed to maintain that unity. Please observe that these are social and corporate virtues; neither love nor longsuffering can be developed in isolation: 'love, joy, peace, longsuffering, gentleness, goodness, faith, meekness, temperance (AV)' are all virtues required in a congregational context. Love demands an object, longsuffering implies others to suffer, and neither meekness nor gentleness can be practised in solitary confinement.

It is not so frequently recognized that the contrasting 'works of the flesh' are also social and corporate sins. We often assume that the list is predominantly sexual (because of the word 'flesh'), and indeed the first three words do describe sexual sins; the next two are 'occult' sins, but most of the rest are what we could call the 'church' sins, namely 'hatred, discord, jealousy, fits of rage, selfish ambition, dissensions, factions, and envy ...' (Gal. 5:19–21). These 'works' are the common accompaniments of controversy and disagreement in the church – and they are sins contrasted with the fruit of the Spirit, sins which destroy the unity of the Spirit. Two of the words used in this list occur significantly, explaining why the divided Corinthian church is 'fleshly' and 'mere infants': 'You are still worldly. For since there is *jealousy* and *quarrelling* among you, are you not worldly?' (1 Cor. 3:3). One of the agonies about differences and dissensions in the church is that the works of the flesh are promoted on both sides of the dispute. Both get angry, both are ready to believe the worst about each other and so on. And it is this bitter-tasting carnal quarrelling that makes so many people disenchanted with their churches today. Since returning from missionary service overseas, I have been astonished at how many Christians are unhappy in their own churches and how many congregations are torn apart by dissension.

The unity of the Spirit is attained through the fruit of the Spirit and hindered by the works of the flesh. Divisiveness is one of the works of the flesh.

The unity of the Spirit is a present reality to be maintained.

2. The church will enjoy the unity of the faith one day in the future

Until we all arrive at the unity of the faith and of the knowledge of the Son of God and become mature, attaining to the whole measure of the fulness of Christ. (Eph. 4:13)

While the unity of the Spirit is a present reality, the unity of the faith is seen as a future goal to be reached. In the context we are told that God gives not only the fruit of the Spirit, but also the gifts of the

Spirit – in the Ephesians context, gifts from Christ to the churches, gifted people serving as apostles, prophets, pastors or teachers, and evangelists: all of them slaves conquered by the victorious king.

> . . . to prepare (equip or perfect) God's people for works of service, so that the body of Christ may be built up until we all reach (attain, arrive at) *unity in the faith* (Eph. 4:12–13a, brackets added).

Unity in the faith is a future goal, not yet attained, and seen as a destination towards which all Christians are moving.

In 1 Corinthians 3 the divided quarrelsome state is regarded as immaturity: the Christians are called 'Mere infants in Christ', while in the future, '. . . we will no longer be infants' (Eph. 4:14), squabbling like children in the ecclesiastical nursery. In addition to this uncomplimentary kindergarten image of the church, the existing situation is seen as being unstable and shifting (rather than rooted and settled), like small boats being whirled about by waves and storms (associated with crafty, deceitful men who deliberately mislead the people of God).

By contrast, maturity is portrayed as a faultlessly functioning body (Eph. 4:16), when all Christians will be perfectly linked to Christ the head and everything will be operating as it ought, each member relating properly to other members.

Unity on earth then, is not a matter of expediency, but the great goal towards which we are all moving.

3. The church glorified in heaven
is one church

Christ loved the Church and gave himself up for her to make her holy, cleansing her by the washing with water through the Word, and to present her to himself as a radiant church, without stain or wrinkle or any other blemish, but holy and blameless (Eph. 5:26–27).

This imagery of the church as a perfected bride is also found in the Revelation, though it must stem from our Lord's description of himself as being the bridegroom.

I saw the Holy City, the New Jerusalem coming down out of heaven from God, prepared as a bride beautifully dressed for her husband. . . . They will be his people, and God himself will be with them and be their God (Rev. 21:2–3).

We shall look further at this subject further of the destiny of the church in chapter 12. For the present it is surely significant that we expect to be a united, perfected church in heaven — not many churches, but one. If this is so, and I am to sit down then in perfect amity with those with whom at present I disagree, this must affect my present attitude towards them. Do we really feel that our denominational divisions are permanent, or do we expect them to disappear as we move towards a heavenly church?

4. New Testament experience of
competing groups

It would be easy to assume that in the New Testament

there are no problems, and to comment, perhaps, that the apostle never seems to have seen secession or separation as a solution to the differences he was writing about. Also, it seems that to Paul unity was assumed. In fact there are a considerable number of references to aspects of disunity in Paul's writing. Some of those who are mentioned are plainly heretics and rogues, deceivers and imposters, while others are manifestly sincere but misguided. The early churches were so far from perfection that nearly all seem to have struggled with problems of disunity. This at least is biblical!

Romans

We will discuss later in this chapter the different views found in the congregations in Rome. But it is worth noting at this point that the book ends with a strong warning:

> I urge you, brothers, to watch out for those who cause divisions and put obstacles in your way that are contrary to the teaching you have learned. Keep away from them. For such people are not serving our Lord Christ, but their own appetites. By smooth talk and flattery, they deceive the minds of naïve people (Rom. 16:17–18).

1 Corinthians

Later in this chapter we will also look at Paul's appeal to the Corinthians not to perpetuate divisions within their congregation. In 1 Corinthians 6 he urges the church to settle its own disputes rather than going to the secular courts (6:1–8). In chapter 8 he deals with a group who use slogans about their own 'knowledge'. This is a commonplace of factions, that they believe themselves to be more enlightened than others, and so are 'puffed up'. If you say to your brother or sister, 'I used to be on three cylinders like you, but now I am on four!', your attitude makes them feel threatened unless they have the maturity to reply – 'Praise God for every blessing, but please remember you have at least sixteen cylinders more to find!' It would be presumptuous to feel that we already know all the blessings with which God has blessed us in Christ Jesus.

Then in chapter 11 Paul writes of the sad social divisions that arise when they eat together (11:17–22) and comments that some of them have not yet grasped the importance of the resurrection (15:12ff.).

2 Corinthians

Paul has problems with those who commend themselves (10:12–18): 'Such men are false apostles, deceitful workmen, masquerading as apostles of Christ' (11:13ff.), and he fears that there are quarrels, jealousy, outbursts of anger, factions, slander, gossip and disorder (12:20).

Galatians

Some people are throwing you into confusion and are trying to pervert the gospel of Christ. ... If anybody is preaching to you a gospel other than what you accepted, let him be eternally condemned! (1:7–9).

and even more strongly:

Those people are zealous to win you over, but for no good. What they want is to alienate you from us, so that you may be zealous for them (4:17–19).

We have already seen that the sins of the flesh in the corporate church context include discord, dissensions and factions (5:22).

Ephesians

Christians are not to be infants, 'blown here and there by every wind of teaching and by the cunning and

craftiness of men in their deceitful scheming' (4:14).
Then in a general epistle (not addressed to any specific
set of church problems) Paul reminds us how common
the problem of immaturity was even then.

Philippians

It is true that some preach Christ out of envy and
rivalry ... out of selfish ambition, not sincerely,
supposing they can stir up trouble for me
(1:15–17).

Many live as enemies of the cross of Christ. ...
Their mind is on earthly things (3:17–19).

Colossians

I tell you this so that no-one may deceive you by
fine-sounding arguments. ... See to it that no-one
takes you captive through hollow and deceptive
philosophy, which depends on human tradition.
... Such a person goes into great detail about what
he has seen, and his unspiritual mind puffs him
up with idle notions ... they are based on human
commands and teachings (2:4, 8, 18, 22).

1 Thessalonians

Not so many problems of this kind appear in this letter,
but the warning not to despise prophecies is followed
by the command to, 'test everything. Hold on to the
good. Avoid every kind of evil' (5:19–22).

2 Thessalonians

It seems that some have spread a false prophecy,
report or letter in the name of the apostles. 'Don't let
anyone deceive you ...'. Later the letter warns of the
danger of counterfeit miracles, signs and wonders
(2:3, 9).

1 Timothy

Timothy has been left behind to 'command certain men not to teach false doctrines any longer nor to devote themselves to myths and endless genealogies. These promote controversies rather than God's work. . . . Some have wandered away from these and turned to meaningless talk' (1:3–6). There are more strong warnings in 4:1–7 but the final chapter is the strongest:

> If anyone teaches false doctrines . . . he is conceited and understands nothing. He has an unhealthy interest in controversies and quarrels about words that result in envy, strife, malicious talk, evil suspicions and constant friction. . .'
> (6:3–5).

This is such an accurate diagnosis of what controversy and division do to even the best Christian people. Interestingly, what follows seems relevant to so-called 'prosperity teaching':

> . . . men of corrupt mind . . . who think that godliness is a means to financial gain. . . . People who want to get rich fall into temptation and a trap and into many foolish and harmful desires. . . . Some people, eager for money, have wandered from the faith and pierced themselves with many griefs (6:5–10).

There is a further warning in 6:20–21.

2 Timothy

> Avoid godless chatter because those who indulge in it will become more and more ungodly. Their teaching will spread like gangrene. . . . Among them are [those] who have wandered away from the truth . . . they destroy the faith of some. . . . Don't have anything to do with foolish and stupid

arguments, because you know they produce quarrels. And the Lord's servant must not quarrel ...' (2:16–18, 23ff.).

The whole passage is instructive in telling us how to deal with such problems and people.

* * *

After all that, we cannot claim that we have not been warned and are without teaching to help us deal with differences and divisions. What conclusions can we draw from all this?

1. The early church in all its freshness and the power of the Spirit was not free from worrying and distasteful competition.

2. We should regard this as a 'normal' and anticipated problem instead of allowing ourselves to be discouraged when we encounter similar things.

3. At the same time we should hold firmly to biblical principles, seek to maintain the unity of the Spirit, and work towards the future attainment of the unity of the faith.

4. We should take every possible opportunity to express our unity in the Spirit now, and desire for unity in the faith in the future, particularly at the grassroots level between local churches, and where there is no compromise implied with fundamental Christian doctrines. Denominational differences are rarely about fundamentals.

5. Christians are commanded to maintain the unity which does exist and to move diligently to that unity which does not yet exist

There are some who shrug their shoulders and say,

'never mind what others are doing, we will get on with building our work, and let others fulfil their calling.' This free-enterprise attitude would be sufficient if we did not have the expectation of a time in the future when 'there will be one flock and one shepherd' (Jn. 10:16). We cannot rest content with a *status quo* situation and ignore one another. 'You do love all the brothers throughout Macedonia. Yet we urge you, brothers, to do so more and more.' (1 Thes. 4:10). They are being pointed to the wider circle of Christians, not merely their own immediate local congregation.

If the 'unity of the faith' is a biblical goal set before us in the Word of God, and Scripture tells us that God has a purpose, a goal, to bring us all together with Christ as head over all, then some response is called for. We cannot merely assent intellectually, but do nothing and leave it to the Lord to arrange events, almost in spite of us and our differences and divisiveness, as though he had never told us what his will is. Are we ultimately to be forced grudgingly and unwillingly into a unity we do not want, with people we disagree with? Or, rather, will we start working towards his goal for us.

We may say: 'Lord, if this really is your will, though I do not see how those Anglican people, or those Pentecostal brethren, for example, can possibly be right, but if you yourself say that it will be so, then I must accept it humbly and obediently. If this is my Lord's will, and you have told me so, how can I stand in the way of it, impede and hinder it or even merely ignore it?' If we will one day sit down side by side in glory, then it must modify (to some extent at least) our present intransigence and suspicion of these other people. We must seek to find common ground in the same Scriptures, to speak together frankly about those areas where we differ and find out why. We must try to do things together when we can.

'That sounds dangerously like ecumenism!' might be your understandable objection. The ecumenical people are not wrong in their perception of the goal, only in their readiness to jettison biblical truths for the sake of visible unity, or to cover over significant differences by the use of ambiguous language. The goal of 'the unity of the faith' is correct: it is a biblical goal. We cannot afford to be divided indefinitely on a basis of past church history. In many parts of the world some national churches are divided from each other, not on the basis of their own past history, but on divisions imported into their countries from the outside. We must try to develop a biblical perspective on our divisions and understand where they fit into God's great purposes for us all.

6. Differences between Christians

The New Testament gives us clear practical guidance in two distinct situations: first, when there are diferences and factions within one single congregation, as at Corinth; and second, when there are differences between neighbouring congregations, as in Rome.

a. Divisions and factions within one local church (1 Cor. 1:10 – 3:23)

After his initial address and customary greetings and opening prayer, Paul moves immediately into the substance of his appeal:

> I appeal to you, brothers, in the name of our Lord Jesus Christ, that all of you agree with one another so that there may be no divisions among you and that you may be perfectly united in mind and thought (1 Cor. 1:10).

Paul is appealing for unity because he has heard of the existence of factions in the congregation, some of whom, to his embarrassment, even claim to be followers

70

of his. The existence of factions within a single church is a situation with which many of us are distressingly familiar these days. Paul's response is very powerful: 'Is Christ divided? Was Paul crucified for you? Were you baptised in the name of Paul?' (1 Cor. 1:13).

It is axiomatic that Christ cannot possibly be divided: there is only the *one* Lord who died for all as the one Saviour and they were baptized either in the name of Jesus (Acts 2:38) or of the Trinity (Mt. 28:19). There is a contrast between those who seek wisdom (Apollos' followers?) and those who seek miracles (Peter's followers?). Paul urges that it is foolish to boast in human leaders and he brands this as being carnal and childish (1 Cor. 3:1–4). Human leaders are 'only servants', those God condescends to use to plant and water churches; but it is God who makes them grow.

Paul follows this explanation with a terrible warning against divisions:

> Don't you know that you yourselves are God's temple and that God's Spirit lives in you? If anyone destroys God's temple, God will destroy him; for God's temple is sacred, and you are that temple (1 Cor. 3:16–17).

Then he goes on to remind them that in fact all human teachers belong to them:

> So then, no more boasting about men! All things are yours, whether Paul or Apollos or Cephas ... all are yours, and you are of Christ, and Christ is of God (1 Cor. 3:21–22).

We are foolish to shut ourselves up within only one narrow Christian tradition or to follow just one human teacher, however excellent. So we must not merely follow the Puritans, tremendous as their theology and their pastoral teaching were; or just charismatic leaders, however stirring they may be; or just radical social theology, despite the needs of today's world. We are very prone to become disciples of human leaders and teachers. All of them are ours, given by God, and we must take what is good, biblical and spiritual, and reject what is unscriptural, distorted and unbalanced.

It is God's church, and therefore, Paul argues, it is foolish to divide on the basis of human teachers and their doctrines and emphases. Division is a struggle between the pathetic fallible humanity of the church, and the reality that it is God's church and not man's.

Why do differences occur? If Scripture were clearer, for example, on how much water should be used and the minimum age of baptismal candidates, then we should know whether to be paedobaptists or credo-baptists! But the Lord has chosen not to tell us this. Paul explains in a significant verse:

> No doubt there have to be differences among you, to show which of you have God's approval (1 Cor. 11:19).

Differences, and the way we handle them, show the reality of our faith. If we adopt a hostile stance, if we slander those we differ from, or if we go and blow our tops, we reveal the truth about our own lack of true spirituality. God has allowed differences to give us the opportunity of manifesting the fruit of the Spirit rather than the works of the flesh. Differences also provide the opportunity of pleasing him and gaining his approval by the way we relate to those from whom we differ.

b. Differences between adjacent congregations (Romans 14–16)

It is interesting to contrast Paul's greeting 'to the church of God in Corinth ... together with those everywhere who call on the name of our Lord Jesus Christ – their Lord and ours' (1 Cor. 1:2) with the address of the letter to the Romans: 'To all in Rome who are loved by God and called to be saints' (Rom. 1:7). Why no address to 'the church of God in Rome'? It seems improbable that in the metropolitan city of the empire there would be only one congregation. As we turn the pages of Romans, we look in vain for the occurrence of the word *ekklēsia*, and we do not meet it until the final chapter, where the word occurs in relation to the local church in Cenchrea (verse 1), all the churches of the Gentiles (verse 3), all the churches of Christ (verse 16), the whole church from where Paul is writing in Corinth (verse 23), and about churches other than in Rome itself.

But there are also references which indicate that several different congregations were meeting together in Rome:

'The church that meets in their house' (Aquila and Priscilla) (Rom. 1:5)
'. . . and the brothers with them' (Asyncritus and four others) (Rom. 1:14)
'. . . all the saints with them' (Philologos and four others) (Rom. 1:15)

It is also possible that the households of Aristobulus, a Jewish group (Rom. 1:10), and of Narcissus (Rom. 1:11) were the focus of other church groups.[1]

The apparent reference to different groups of Christians in the various quarters of the city is especially interesting when we examine the different attitudes of Roman Christians to eating meat, observing the sabbath and drinking, in chapter 14. Some ate only vegetables, others felt free to eat meat. Some esteemed all days alike, others observed the sabbath. If we put these facts together we can see that congregations in the Jewish quarter would almost certainly observe the sabbath, and would not eat non-kosher meat. In the Asian quarter or the Italian quarter Christians might well have no scruples about food, and would never have kept the Jewish sabbath. In one quarter one ethnic subculture would be dominant, and in another, a different one. It would then be possible to have different practices in different congregations. But what when they wanted to meet on a Saturday, or when they wanted to eat together? Were the Jews to scrap their scruples, or were the Gentiles to curtail their liberty in order not to offend their fellow Christians?

> It is better not to eat meat or drink wine, or do anything else that will cause your brother to fall (Rom. 14:21).

The tense used here does not mean that habitually they will never again enjoy their liberty; but that on specific occasions when a brother or sister might be caused to stumble, they will abstain, and keep their liberty a secret between them and God (verse 22). The stress of the passage is seen as:

> Accept (*i.e.* welcome) one another (verse 1) . . . for God has accepted you (verse 3) . . . accept one another . . . just as Christ accepted you (15:7).

Their differences are not to be allowed to keep them apart, and so Paul prays that the God who gives endurance and encouragement would give:

> . . . *a spirit of unity* among yourselves as you follow Christ Jesus, so that with one heart and mouth you may glorify the God and Father of our Lord Jesus Christ (15:5–6).

Notice this further important biblical reference to 'unity' in addition to the two we have already considered in Ephesians 4.

Conclusion

These two passages in Corinthians and Romans, taken seriously, give clear guidelines to believers who differ from one another in the same congregation, and in different congregations with differing convictions. It is not merely that it would be nice and pleasant for Christians to get on well with those they differ from – there are profound biblical and theological reasons for pursuing unity. We cannot blandly continue our present differences and denominations as if they enjoyed some permanent status or sanction from God. They arise from the humanness of the church, and the Bible describes factions as carnal and childish, as marks of spiritual immaturity. They arise because now we know only in part and prophesy in part (1 Cor. 13:9) and see in a glass darkly (1 Cor. 13:12).

But Scripture is crystal clear that our ultimate destination is the 'unity of the faith' and therefore we must now 'maintain the unity of the Spirit' and pray for a 'spirit of unity' among ourselves. We need to live in the light of this truth, to embrace it, delight in it and praise God for it. *We all need to take a fresh look at the way we in our own local church relate to other local churches. To be aware of their existence is surely not sufficient.*

Now that the significance of the local church has been so widely recognized and generally emphasized, we need, over the next decade, to see a more realistic attempt to grapple with what 'all one in Christ Jesus' ought to mean at the local-church level. Paul wrote to the Thessalonians about their brotherly love for one another, and then said 'In fact you do love all the brothers throughout Macedonia. Yet we urge you, brothers, to do so more and more' (1 Thes. 4:10).

DIMENSIONS OF CHURCH GROWTH: QUANTITATIVE AND QUALITATIVE

(Use this as a checklist to measure progress in your church.)

A. *Quantitative*

1. Growth in numbers of Christians (Acts 2:41; 5:14; 6:7).
2. Growth in numbers of congregations (Acts 16:5).

B. *Qualitative (1 Cor. 3:12–13; Eph.4:12–13).*

3. Growth in love and interpersonal relations (1 Thes. 4:10; 1 Pet.1:22; 4:8).
4. Growth in congregational co-operation as a body (Eph. 4:16).
5. Growth in training and sending teachers (Acts 11:25; 13:1–2; 15:35).
6. Growth in congregational profile (Eph. 5:21–22; 6:4).
7. Growth in holiness and beautiful lifestyle (2 Cor. 3:18; Eph. 5:27).
8. Growth in congregational impact on society (1 Pet. 2:12; 1 Thes. 1:8).
9. Growth in doctrinal understanding and education (Col. 1:28; 1 Cor. 14:20).
10. Growth in reality of worship together (Eph. 5:18–20; Col. 3:15–16).
11. Growth in sacrificial giving (2 Cor. 8:1–5).
12. Growth in commitment to worldwide mission (Rom. 15:30; Col. 4:12–13).

chapter five
THE GROWTH OF THE CHURCH
How does it grow?

Introduction

Our longing for the perfecting of the church means that we look for growth and development in our congregations in many different ways.

Because the church is human and fallible there is room for growth. Over-emphasis upon its divine aspect, upon justification, so that we are considered to be already perfect, may hinder recognition of the need for growth within a self-satisfied, subcultural ghetto-church.

It is God who gives the growth (1 Cor. 3:7) and therefore we shall be rightly suspicious of human methodologies of church growth that give us a certain prescription for human activity that will automatically make the churches grow. When God is working in sovereign power, whether very rapidly in revival or more gradually through normal church activity, he will work, whatever current methodology is in vogue. But any consideration of church growth and church-planting must relate to some kind of ecclesiology or theology of the church.

Those of us with missionary experience have worked not only in pioneer church-planting situations but also in places where strong indigenous churches have come into existence and where there is still a great deal of work to be done. Some people call this church-perfecting, others church renewal. There is always a need for the constant quickening of existing churches, already planted, but in need of establishing, strengthening and pruning to enable them to grow properly.

Both church-planting and church-perfecting alike are forms of church growth, one being initial and primary and the other subsequent and secondary: but both are essential to the task of a perfected glorious church without spot or blemish. Church growth may be both quantitative and qualitative, and both forms of growth are significant for initial church-planting and consequent church-perfecting.

Church re-planting

Christians with a strong sense of historical continuity and loyalty to the establishment[1] may feel that in northern European countries with a Protestant tradition, church renewal is more appropriate than planting new congregations.

The pioneer missionary, on the other hand, is usually trying to plant Christian churches in a virgin area as far as Christianity is concerned. It is rarely a religious desert, though it may be dense virgin jungle thick with indigenous superstition and pagan religious beliefs, perhaps more developed into Hindu or Islamic systems, but needing the light of the good news of Jesus Christ. There is, however, no sense of any competition with other Christian churches: there is room for all to plant churches in such spiritual wildernesses.

But others may be starting all over again to plant churches in some country with an established Roman Catholic or institutional Protestant church system, perhaps with an established system of parishes. This is more like trying to plant new congregations in an existing plantation – though the spaces between congregations may be so great that there is not really any competition. However, there could well be some denominational friction or hostility. In the past, systems of church 'comity' meant that various missions agreed to assign areas of work to different groups in such a way that they did not compete directly with one another. In recent years most missions have abandoned comity agreements in major mushrooming city areas, because everyone agrees there is so much work to be done. But this is not the situation in Britain and other Protestant countries of western and northern Europe.

Anyone wanting to plant new churches in Britain or Germany is trying to plant in a garden already over-planted with denominational shrubs! Many trees and bushes have been there for years, though some are dead or dying. There is understandable hostility, even xenophobia, against 'American missions' or 'splinter sects' who try to plant a new church of their own variety in the middle of this already densely packed denominational shrubbery. Looking after an existing garden is different from starting a new one. If some plants die off after a severe winter or a summer drought, there will be space for something new. If one plant is old or sparse you may decide to root it out to make room for a new plant full of fresh vigour. In such areas it might be better to speak of church re-planting, rather than simply church-planting.

However, as indicated in chapter 2, we must not despise the church of God and ignore older churches merely because they are older! Even with the 5% church attendance that is average for some rural areas of Britain, church re-planting is likely to be regarded as schismatic, sectarian, intolerant and many other un-British things! The same would certainly be true in rural Scandinavia or Germany. Some people like Canon John Poulton of Norwich, are visionary enough to believe, 'that many of our answers in terms of the future of the church in the villages will only be found together, as Christians of all churches work towards them.'[2] We should work for a greater co-operative breaking down of denominational barriers at ground level.

Three forms of church re-planting

a. Denominational outreach

The established or state church or other longstanding denominational cause may decide to develop daughter churches on some new housing estates. The Baptist churches in Scotland in recent years have nearly all had projects to develop new daughter congregations, often with great success. I know an Anglican church which ten years ago had a congregation of thirty people, and now has five hundred members in three separate congregations and is planting a fourth on a nearby estate.

This seems to be a form of natural growth, like 'layering' an existing shrub so that a new plant develops still attached to the parent shrub, until it is strong enough to have a new life of its own. This may perhaps be regarded by some as legitimate, as opposed to illegitimate growth, where there is no obvious father or mother church on the immediate scene. Such growth from existing churches should be encouraged, provided the mother church does not try to continue treating her growing daughter as a child long after she can stand on her own feet.

b. Spontaneous outstep

This is usually a desperate measure by frustrated Christians indigenous to the local community, who have made every effort to see their church renewed, but have been made to feel unwelcome, or who feel that their children are not being taught and so withdraw to start a new fellowship. Sometimes this may be the product of a personality conflict, justified by exaggerating the significance of some doctrinal difference. Often it may be frustrated impatience with the lack of vision or 'stick-in-the-mud' attitudes of local leadership. It is a 'step out' of some from an existing congregation to form a new group in the same locality.

If it is true that new churches are more vigorous and grow faster than old ones, then perhaps it may increase the number of Christians, as long as it is not merely transfer growth from one group to another. It does not seem that it ought to be encouraged. Writing to the Corinthians the apostle pointedly calls them 'the church of God in Corinth' and it never seems to be a possible option that the factions supporting Peter, Paul and Apollos should split off to form new congregations.

c. Organized outside inpush

Where Christian churches are few and far between, where there is no viable indigenous church, or only an apostate one, such pioneer work may be essential. In fact, truly apostate churches that positively deny some major cardinal doctrine like the deity of Christ or the resurrection are very rare, but there are more that seem spiritually moribund, cold and lacking credibility. However, when there are already existing national churches, such inpush without consultation with, or consideration for existing Christian churches seems unfortunate. It is essentially partisan and sectarian, usually with some new doctrinal emphasis, often regarding itself as authentic, but despising existing churches as unenlightened, inferior and, at best, second-class.

There are huge cities and neglected towns too, where fresh ground could be broken and new congregations planted, without any need to draw people away from existing congregations. If our concern is for the glory of God, and the extending of his kingdom, we cannot adopt some dog-in-the-manger attitude towards fresh growth and outreach. However, in small densely planted 'shrubberies', there is a great danger that in starting a new congregation, existing churches will be weakened by some parasitic transfer growth – 'sheep-stealing' in fact.

Having said this, we have to face the fact that many now respectable and accepted congregations were started in the teeth of most bitter opposition from the establishment: the Congregationalists, the Baptists, the Methodists, the Brethren and the Pentecostals in turn, all came into existence in this way. Most of them initially did (and probably still do) consider themselves to be more enlightened and biblical than the misguided and moribund churches that were there already. Recent developments may be seen only as the latest eruption of something that has happened many times before. It is not therefore necessarily wrong. Those on both sides need to treat the others as *bona fide* Christians, answerable to the same master, and as true congregations of believers. They may be nominal, formal, misguided, liberal and inconsistent at present. But if our concern is for the name of Christ, then we must long for the blessing of the existing churches, as well. Blessing that comes not by their pulling out and joining us, but because of a true quickening of the Holy Spirit within their own ranks.

What kind of growth and what kind of church?

What are 'God's plans' for the church? Those building new empires of their own, piously describe their work as 'what God is doing'. They may be right, but some niggling doubts remain as to what the Lord thinks of it all. We have seen that it is wrong to talk as though God is interested only in novelties, and blesses new churches and writes off old ones. This impugns the faithfulness of God.

What kind of a church is most pleasing to God? We cannot merely be pragmatic, shrug our shoulders, wash our hands and say that any kind of growth is good by church growth standards. We must endeavour to define the kind of churches we plant in biblical terms.

How do all our church divisions, old and new, seem when seen from a heavenly viewpoint? As already mentioned in the chapter on the unity of the church, are we not all seen as immature, carnal and childish?

The dimensions of church growth

a. Quantitative

1. Growth in numbers of Christians
(Acts 2:41; 5:14; 6:7)

You cannot build the new temple without adding to the number of living stones. Acts contains five accounts of individual conversions[3] and three separate accounts of Saul's own conversion. The missionary has always needed to be an evangelist before he could become a teacher. Such growth can be measured in terms of professions of conversion (numbers of decisions), or perhaps more realistically in the number of adult baptisms. This immediately raises the issue of the meaningfulness of decisions, the reality of professions and the quality of discipleship of those who are baptized, so that the need for some *qualitative* assessment even of quantitative growth is obvious.

2. Growth in numbers of congregations
(Acts 16:5)

It is not enough to save souls and baptize bodies, for they must be built together into new visible congregations. Some para-church groups have been weak at this point, with literature distribution or short-term evangelism that measures success only in terms of individual conversions, without seeing the importance of the congregation as a viable unit. It is not that God is unable to keep individual converts alive and well in a lonely situation without fellowship or teaching, but that it is not his usual plan. The body illustration does not presuppose keeping limbs and organs alive in tissue culture apart from a living body of believers.

There is so much church-planting still to be done, so many countries where Christians are a tiny minority and churches only to be found in major cities. There are whole *départements* (like counties) in France with no evangelical congregations at all. In Kampuchea there were only twenty-seven congregations and most of them in the capital Pnomh Penh when that city fell in 1975 Christians are forbidden to meet there at present. And Kampuchea is a country with a population greater than Scotland or Switzerland.

The great failure of European missionary societies has been their failure to continue a church-planting ministry owing to ecumenical lack of conviction that Christ is the only way of salvation. Too many of the popular ancillary 'missions' have misdirected the focus of the Christian public away from church-planting to worthy, but less significant work.

The history of Acts gives us a biblical pattern for mission; the apostolic missionaries spent their energies preaching the gospel, saving souls, baptizing converts and planting churches. Acts tells us that what matters most is that new congregations of Christians should be started in every place. Somehow Christians and churches today seem for the most part to have lost that overriding concern and vision, although there are some glorious exceptions.

b. Qualitative (1 Cor. 3:12–13; Eph. 4:12–13)

If perchance the church should attract men without at the same time transforming them; if she shall attach them to her membership without assimilating them to her life, she has only weakened herself by her increase and diminished herself by her addition. (A. J. Gordon)

A church of one hundred half-hearted members grows to become a church of two hundred half-hearted members: there is quantitative growth without corresponding qualitative growth. There has been huge numerical gowth in parts of Indonesia, where the Pantya Cila ('Five Points' of the Constitution) gives first place to 'reverence for Godhead'. Animists are encouraged to embrace a monotheistic faith – Islam or Christianity. But if you want to go on eating pork, you had better become a Christian, not a Muslim. This quality of 'convert' may mean large congregations, but the quality of commitment to Christ, or experience of 'new birth' is open to question.

It is not enough to increase the number of bricks or even the number of piles of bricks. Those bricks must be built into a permanent building, strong and beautifully constructed. In the same way, a body is quite different from a large pile of minced meat – it is a living body made up of members that relate to one another and function together. So when we speak about church growth we are not concerned only with dimensions of body mass, how large and gross the body is, but also with considerations of health, physique, muscle tone and co-ordination. If Cinderella has ataxia it means that she lacks this aspect of normal healthy growth.

Evangelicals and ecumenicals alike have neglected this aspect of church growth. Ecumenicals have reacted against evangelical criticism of institutionalism and nominalism, while some evangelicals have placed so much emphasis upon evangelism that they have, until recent years, been less concerned about the quality of congregational life.

3. Growth in love and interpersonal relations (1 Thes. 4:10; 1 Pet. 1:22; 4:8)

The epistles are packed with commands that love between the members of churches should increase more and more. Peter's first letter returns to this theme repeatedly (1:22; 2:17; 3:8; 4:8). Paul says explicitly that 'the whole body . . . grows and builds itself up in love' (Eph 4:16). His famous chapter on spiritual gifts and the way in which Christians function together as a body (1 Cor. 13) reminds the Corinthians that while spiritual gifts will ultimately be redundant, the fruit of the Spirit, which is love, is eternally part of heaven.

The notion of a 'drive-in' church, found in parts of the United States, where you attend without having to meet anyone, is an obscenity. Christians are expected to relate to each other in an ever-growing relationship of mutual concern and love.

Congregations may grow, progress from formality, the artificiality of purely formal greetings, to genuine interpersonal relationships in the household (or family) of God where friends know *philadelphia*, the love of brothers and sisters. That does not mean treating others *as though* they were your brothers and sisters, but recognizing that in Christ they *are* your brothers and sisters.

4. Growth in congregational co-operation as a body (Eph. 4:16)

A body may grow and develop in relation to the extent that its members cease to be passive spectators and become actively involved participators in the life of the congregation. A body in which only one member is functioning is almost dead and is taken off to hospital in hope that the total function may be restored. The one-man-band concept of the church is a cultural hang-over from the days when the squire and parson, or the laird and minister, were the only literate people in the parish capable of reading Scripture or the prayers. Roy Castle is credited in the *Guinness Book of Records* with playing thirty different musical instruments in three minutes: what an illustration of the omnicompetent one-man-band minister who sees himself as a soloist and not a conductor.

So often a majority of church members are passive spectators and less than 10% are really active. There is a 'collusion in dependence' (an expression I owe to David Pawson), for lazy church members like to leave it to the minister, and the individualistic minister prefers doing it all himself: it's much less bother than training others to do it! Theological education needs to give far more thought to the training of ministers who will see their chief task to be trainers and motivators of others, conductors of the congregational orchestra not pulpit prima donnas.

There has been some advance into 'team ministry', but this may be little improvement on the North American church pattern of a team of very professional ministers, each paid for a different function such as pastoral counselling, music, youth ministries, or Christian education. The ordinary layperson still does not get a look in: he is still the spectator who pays others to perform.

A congregation, then, makes real progress in involving an increasing number in some form of ministry. A good example of involvement is Guildford Baptist Church where more than 300 members had specific jobs to do at one time. This view of 'body life' or 'shared ministry' is an important dimension of growth. The ministers are not unemployed: the heart must pump blood to the other members, the steersman helps direct the ship while the oarsmen pull. In the Far East recently I heard a comparison between the 'sampan' minister, where one man paddles the whole boat along single-handed, and the 'dragonboat' or 'war-canoe' pastor, who ensures that every other man on board is paddling in a perfect rhythm of energy – and what rapid progress results.

5. Growth in training and sending teachers (Acts 11:25; 13:1-2; 15:35)

The Antioch congregation gives us a classical example here. Barnabas was sent by the Jerusalem church to take charge of the new, rapidly growing congregation in Antioch, third city of the Roman empire. Some of those Christians scattered from Jerusalem were following the precedent set by Peter in Caesarea in preaching to Gentiles. Not long after arriving there he headed northwards from Syria into Cilicia to seek out Saul in Tarsus. He brought him back to Antioch and together they taught the congregation for a year, by which time there were five named teaching prophets. There was also a readiness to hear the Holy Spirit telling them to send off two teachers to become 'apostles' on the first missionary journey. When they returned from their church-planting in Galatia, and from the Council in Jerusalem, it is clear that there were more than five people involved in teaching: 'they and many others taught and preached the word of the Lord' (15:35). Barnabas did not settle down to a one-man ministry, but his ministry led to a multiplication of gifted teachers in Antioch itself, and they were now equipped to take the gospel to other places. Next he sets off with Mark for Cyprus, and Paul with Silas for Asia Minor.

It is by this kind of teacher-multiplying ministry that one church is enabled to send out workers from among those they have trained themselves, to plant new churches elsewhere. Such methods may be found today: a very unselfish missionary in South Thailand trained five men in two years to preach and accept pastoral responsibility. One had left school early at sixteen, the others had only primary education. None of them could have left their farms and stopped supporting their families to go to Bible college; but they were all trained on the spot by a man who felt that he was 'not much of a preacher and teacher', and so was willing to give the local Christians both training and opportunities to preach and teach.

An interesting work at a commuter university in Sydney encourages those who are seeking to attend classes for seekers, then classes for young converts, and then classes where they learn to evangelize. After that they go on to a class which trains them to run teaching groups for seekers, for young converts, and for evangelists. By this time they have become full-time assistants in the church, which leads to many going on to theological college. This example illustrates how increasing the number of teachers is an important form of church growth.

6. Growth in congregational profile (Eph. 5:21–22; 6:4)

In Asia you can have whole congregations of teenagers or unmarried young people in their twenties. Some new churches in Singapore have two or three hundred members, but only two or three married couples. I know of similar churches in the Philippines and in North Japan. It is good to see so many young people, but a local church should be socially comprehensive in its membership. Paul, writing to the Ephesian church, addresses 'wives . . . husbands . . . children' (Eph. 5:21–22; 6:4).

Such congregations progress as young people marry and start new Christian homes, so that the church develops a profile more representative of the population as a whole. Some British churches with a huge majority of elderly people need to see themselves rejuvenated by reaching out to younger people. This whole growth in congregational profile is important growth. It may be that there is a majority of women: men are outnumbered in many churches by two to one and in others by as many as six to one.[4]

A church then may grow by coming closer to the profile of the population in a balance between old and young, male and female, married and unmarried, and also in being representative of different races and classes in the population as a whole.

7. Growth in holiness and beautiful lifestyle (2 Cor. 3:18; Eph. 5:27)

Sanctification in the New Testament is more often corporate and congregational than solitary. 'We all' beholding as in a mirror the glory of the Lord, are being changed into his likeness. The appeal of Paul to the Romans to present themselves to God (12:1–2) is an appeal to them as 'brethren', as a congregation of saints. The very word 'saints' occurs some sixty-one times in the plural and only once in the singular, 'Greet every saint' (Phil. 4:21 AV) where its meaning is clearly plural also! The fruit of the Spirit is also corporate: love and longsuffering alike demand other Christians to love and suffer long.

It is not a few individual stained-glass window saints God wants, but whole saintly congregations whose corporate lifestyle is testimony to the reality of the God who transfigures their corporate daily lives.

Congregations can grow cold and backslide just as individuals can and do. There have been mass turnings to Christ where there has never been a clear renunciation of animistic customs and fetishes, where morality has never yet been recalibrated to biblical standards. It was in congregations like this that revival broke out in Borneo and in North Thailand in the seventies: in both cases whole congregations repented, destroyed their compromising charms, and were cleansed and filled afresh with God's Holy Spirit.

This dimension is often missed: congregations as a whole making progress in holy living, with beautiful lives that shine, like a city set on a hill which cannot be hidden for its blazing light.

8. Growth in congregational impact on society (1 Pet. 2:12; 1 Thes. 1:8)

Paul suggests three interesting corporate images for the church in Phil. 1:27: living like citizens (*politeuesthe*), fighting like soldiers (*stēkete*) and striving together side by side like a team of gladiators or athletes (*synathlountes*). In civic responsibilities Christians are to have an influence like salt, preserving society. Christians are coming increasingly under attack where moral matters are concerned. A biblical stand against homosexual practice, for instance, will mean accusations of discrimination on the grounds of sexual orientation; an insistence that Christ alone can save will make us suspected of racial intolerance.

Paul's athletic metaphor sees the team united in moving together with a common purpose, in the face of opposition. They pass opportunities to one another, they back each other up as they press home their attack. All three metaphors show that the church grows as it goes out into the world, serving together in evangelism and outreach, in good works, and perhaps even social protest, when necessary.

In doing things together as Christians, the church grows stronger. It grows by doing, and especially by doing things which are a blessing to others in society as a whole. Sadly it is true that some congregations have little or no local impact; they might as well not be there. Others, however, have considerable impact. This then is another kind of growth: from being an irrelevant ghetto-church, to one which makes an impact and has a beneficial effect upon society.

9. Growth in doctrinal understanding and education (Col. 1:28; 1 Cor. 14:20)

Sadly there are some congregations which are theologically clueless and biblically illiterate. Churches can be ineffective in teaching the members Christian truth. At London Bible College, we regularly administer tests of biblical knowledge to applicants, and are appalled at how little some Christians actually know of the Bible. Some churches hop about the Bible at random, a process of serendipity, without any systematic teaching in the church of any kind (except perhaps of small children in the Sunday school). Our school system no longer teaches the Christian faith as it used to do: Christianity is one option among many, which is all the more ironic as Muslims would never permit Islam to be so disregarded in a country where they were in the majority. But churches are often so bad at systematic teaching.

Church members are fed, if that is the right word, on haphazard and hastily prepared devotional snacks thrown together at the last minute, more the product of professional desperation to have something to say than as part of any clearly defined programme of teaching. Such churches suffer from doctrinal malnutrition and dietary deficiency. Compared with secular teaching in schools it can all be so amateurish and vague.

There is room here again for growth and progress in tackling the whole process of instructing a congregation thoroughly in all the great doctrines of the faith, in teaching them the whole counsel of God, and giving them an overall grasp of the whole of Scripture and its relevance to modern daily life. In the Bible, 'knowledge' and 'wisdom' are not merely cerebral and intellectual, but experimental and devotional.

Christians must press their church leaders for teaching. In these days when many enrol for courses by correspondence, even to degreee level, it is worth remembering that good Christian correspondence course material is also available. But this is no substitute for good church teaching, and we can learn better in groups. Some American churches offer a variety of options quarter by quarter so that adults can study and learn the Scriptures. It is high time we saw that this is one of the most important reasons why Christians ought to meet together – for mutual upbuilding.

There is vast scope for growth and progress in this dimension.

10. Growth in reality of worship together (Eph. 5:18–20; Col. 3:15–16)

In recent years great progress has been made in this direction, though rather less in Wales, Scotland and Ireland than in England. The pattern is very uneven. The Christian Brethren have always had the opportunity for free, spontaneous worship, as the meeting pursued a theme from Scripture, reinforced by hymns and rich in prayer. Sadly even this can degenerate into formality and the extemporaneous is not necessarily free from cliché. The best assemblies, especially where the priesthood of both men and women is recognized and all may participate, still have a pattern which other churches need.

Charismatic worship can also be real and spontaneous, though it too can degenerate when it is led too much from the front (so that it's not much better than the old song-leader concept), and is little more than a string of unrelated choruses. The identification of chorus singing with 'worship' needs to be challenged. But where there is a sensitive combination of prayerful preparation with opportunity for spontaneous participation, and *appropriate* choruses are used to express response to God speaking in Scripture, there can be authentic worship through the Holy Spirit.

Those who select choruses for publication need to discriminate more both doctrinally and in eliminating banal sentiment. Choruses lack the balance of the psalms, which are not by any means all glad rejoicing, for the Lord is Lord whatever our mood, and may be worshipped when we are sad and depressed (as the Psalmist was sometimes). We do not have to work one another up into a feeling of gladness by hand-clapping in order to start worshipping. It is not easy to find choruses that relate to specific biblical passages as it is to find hymns. The provision of a Scripture index is helpful, but often shows from what a limited selection of scriptures songs are being written. Recent chorus-hymns like 'The Servant King' and 'Meekness and Majesty' are a real blessing and enable us to respond to biblical teaching.

The obsession of some choruses with the 'I lift my hands up...' syndrome is unbalanced, when one remembers that there is only one New Testament reference to it (and there the emphasis is more on the descriptions 'holy' and 'without anger or disputing' [1 Tim. 2:8]). The Lord Jesus also lifted his hands in blessing (Lk. 24:50). I had always assumed that there must be many references in the Psalms, but even there I have only found one reference to *people* clapping their hands (Ps. 47:1) and only six to lifting or stretching out one's hands (Ps. 28:2; 63:4; 88:9; 134:2; 141:2 and 143:6). Only three of these are in praise situations, the others being calls for help, cries of distress or grief. Personally there are times when I want to express lifting up my heart or soul (more frequent biblical expressions), so I am not against the practice as such, but it is out of biblical proportion when it becomes a kind of Masonic secret sign of belonging to an in-group.

The tragedy is that there should be polarization, such as that between hymns and choruses or between psalms and hymns in the Scottish churches (aren't metrical psalms paraphrases just like many hymns?). In spite of claims to inspiration ('The Lord gave me this chorus' – by people who also claim copyright on what would seem to belong to the Lord!), choruses and hymns are attempts to express divine truth in human words. Some do it marvellously, and some do it very badly. We should accept the good and reject the bad, and weigh and judge such human efforts in the light of Scripture. We should try and use all that is worthy as means to worship, and we should not confuse the means with the end.

The word 'adore' seems overworked, though it is difficult to find it in any biblical concordance that I know. The Lord is so vigorous and great, and some of our expressions seem so sloppily sentimental, that I frequently find myself wondering whether he appreciates them very much. Prophetic denunciations of popular worship are remarkably common in Scripture:

> 'I hate, I despise your religious feasts;
>   I cannot stand your assemblies.
> Even though you bring me . . . offerings,
>   I will not accept them.
> Away with the noise of your songs!
>   I will not listen to the music of your harps!
> But let justice roll on like a river,
>   righteousness like a never-failing stream!'
> (Am. 5:21–24)

Here is warning that assembling to worship is not automatically pleasing to the Lord. He wants the worship of the heart, not just the lips. There is a purely carnal, human elation in a large number singing together that should not be equated with worshipping in spirit or truth. Closing of eyes may be no more than subcultural imitation.

It is possible to doze or dream one's way through church services, to obey instructions from the front like obedient sheep, while one's conscious mind is only partly involved. We may sing hymns without feeling a thing, suddenly realizing in the last verse that we have not sung with any understanding or communicated with God or with others. There are other times when every word seems potent with meaning and feeling. Reality is experienced when we progress from a few people being actively engaged in participation some of the time, to a majority exercising their wills to be energetically and meaningfully singing, praying and listening most of the time. This is an area where each person can participate more and more, so that more and more of the congregation are expending energy in spiritual concentration: then there is a hushed quiet of

95

awe that is almost palpable, a spontaneous joy that you can see in opened eyes. This is the kind of growth in congregational participation we must pray for.

There is much to encourage us: people are getting out of the rut of merely going through the motions (and suddenly realizing that they have done it all as automatically as getting dressed in the morning!) and are attempting to progress and grow in reality. But even the best, most sincere exponents have a long way to go. The humanity of the church is never more clearly seen than when we attempt to worship God together!

11. Growth in sacrificial giving (2 Cor. 8:1–5)

Paul commends the Macedonians for their giving, as a challenge to the Achaian Greeks further south to follow their example. He says of them:

> they gave as much as they were able . . . and even beyond their ability . . . they gave themselves first to the Lord, and then to us . . .

The rapid fall-off in British young people offering for long-term missionary work suggests that many have been contaminated with materialism and desire for earthly security, and are less willing to give themselves than their predecessors. The average church giving for the year 1982–83 according to the *UK Christian Handbook* averaged £1.25 per week per church member or £65 per year, little more than the cost of a television licence then! Since the average yearly income was several times more than £650 per year, the majority of Christians were clearly not tithing – giving 10% of their income – to the church. This does not compare very favourably with the generosity of the Macedonian Christians.

Ironically one could comment that giving can be quantified, and that it does give some measurable indication of Christian commitment. If the figure quoted above is in any way accurate, we must be discouraged. It would be better to look at such figures for a single congregation. St Philip and St Jacob Anglican church in Bristol gave £79 to missionary support in 1964, £8,054 in 1973 and £67,976 in 1983.[5] That represents substantial growth in sacrificial giving, but it also reflects a 416% growth in membership of the church, and a Macedonian-like commitment to the service of Christ.

So while it is a qualitative form of church growth it is at the same time something that is measurable. We do well in each congregation both to compare ourselves with others (as Paul made odious comparisons with the Macedonians!) but also to compare ourselves with ourselves. Some churches are hard hit by unemployment or have many students or pensioners who gave generously according to their means, while others may have many wealthy people, who could afford to give much more. We should also consider *how* we give. 'Collections', when they consist of dropping a bit of loose change into a plate, may be a wasteful means of giving in countries where there are government-approved schemes of tax refunding on 'covenanted' charitable giving.

12. Growth in commitment to worldwide mission (Rom. 15:30; Col. 4:12–13)

We have already seen how the Antioch church increased its numbers of teachers and sent its first two teachers out as missionary apostles. Every congregation must ask how many short-term and long-term missionaries it is producing, and how many are in ancillary ministries, and how many in long-term, frontline evangelism and church-planting work. St Helen's, Bishopsgate, in London, draws members from three large teaching hospitals. But its Rector Dick Lucas is hesitant to describe medical workers overseas as 'missionaries', preferring to reserve that title for evangelists and church-planters. Churches need to pray together about which of their own number would be qualified to be sent out in such capacities.

But Paul, writing to the Romans, sees that mission commitment is not something restricted to those who actually go themselves. He writes:

> I urge you, brothers, by our Lord Jesus Christ and by the love of the Spirit, *to join me in my struggle by praying to God for me* (Rom. 15:30).

He is endeavouring to enlist the prayer support of a church he has never yet visited, seeing that their prayer involvement is an important form of mission commitment in the local church, by Christians who may never be called to cross a cultural barrier themselves. Prayer is the purest form of evangelism there is, because it is God who is at work and all the glory is his. Every church member can participate actively in mission through praying.

Every congregation, then, can grow in this dimension – from a church where a few fringe 'fanatics' pray for missionaries, to a church where an increasing number of the central core-members are emotionally and spiritually involved in praying for, giving to and communicating with missionaries in the field.

Conclusion

There are many different ways in which a congregation can progress, and we need to take a list like the one at the beginning of this chapter and pray through it together as a congregation. Even though growth may be qualitative, and therefore not readily quantified, we can make qualitative judgments also: we know whether we can improve and make progress. If we *want* to make progress, we can ask the Lord to work in us all to make it possible.

chapter six

THE PRACTICE OF THE CHURCH

What happens when it meets?

They devoted themselves to the apostles' teaching and to the fellowship, to the breaking of bread and to prayer. (Acts 2:42)

Until I come, devote yourself to the public reading of Scripture, to preaching and to teaching. (1 Tim. 4:13)

Follow the way of love and eagerly desire spiritual gifts, especially the gift of prophecy. For anyone who speaks in a tongue does not speak to men but to God. Indeed, no-one understands him; he utters mysteries with his spirit. But everyone who prophesies speaks to men for their strengthening, encouragement and comfort. He who speaks in a tongue edifies himself, but he who prophesies edifies the church. I would like every one of you to speak in tongues, but I would rather have you prophesy. He who prophesies is greater than one who speaks in tongues, unless he interprets, so that the church may be edified.

Now, brothers, if I come to you and speak in tongues, what good will I be to you, unless I bring you some revelation or knowledge or prophecy or word of instruction? Even in the case of lifeless things that make sounds, such as the flute or harp, how will anyone know what tune is being played unless there is a distinction in the notes? Again, if the trumpet does not sound a clear call, who will get ready for battle? So it is with you. Unless you speak intelligible words with your tongue, how will anyone know what you are saying? You will just be speaking into the air. Undoubtedly there are all sorts of languages in the world, yet none of them is without meaning. If then I do not grasp the meaning of what someone is saying, I am a foreigner to the speaker, and he is a foreigner to me. So it is with you. Since you are eager to have spiritual gifts, try to excel in gifts that build up the church.

For this reason anyone who speaks in a tongue should pray that he may interpret what he says. For if I pray in a tongue, my spirit prays, but my mind is unfruitful.

So what shall I do? I will pray with my spirit, but I will also pray with my mind; I will sing with my spirit, but I will also sing with my mind. If you are praising God with your spirit, how can one who finds himself among those who do not understand say 'Amen' to your thanksgiving, since he does not know what you are saying? You may be giving thanks well enough, but the other man is not edified.

I thank God that I speak in tongues more than all of you. But in the church I would rather speak five intelligible words to instruct others than ten thousand words in a tongue.

Brothers, stop thinking like children. In regard to evil be infants, but in your thinking be adults. In the Law it is written:

'Through men of strange tongues
    and through the lips of foreigners
I will speak to this people,
    but even then they will not listen to me,'
says the Lord.

Tongues, then, are a sign, not for believers but for unbelievers; prophecy, however, is for believers, not for unbelievers. So if the whole church comes together and everyone speaks in tongues, and some who do not understand or some unbelievers come in, will they not say that you are out of your mind? But if an unbeliever or someone who does not understand comes in while everybody is prophesying, he will be convinced by all that he is a sinner and will be judged by all, and the secrets of his heart will be laid bare. So he will fall down and worship God, exclaiming, 'God is really among you!'

What then shall we say, brothers? When you come together, everyone has a hymn, or a word of instruction, a revelation, a tongue or an interpretation. All of these must be done for the strengthening of the church. If anyone speaks in a tongue, two — or at the most three — should speak, one at a time, and someone must interpret. If there is no interpreter, the speaker should keep quiet in the church and speak to himself and God.

Two or three prophets should speak, and the others should weigh carefully what is said. And if a revelation comes to someone who is sitting down, the first speaker should stop. For you can all prophesy in turn so that everyone may be instructed and encouraged. The spirits of prophets are subject to the control of prophets. For God is not a God of disorder but of peace.

As in all the congregations of the saints, women should remain silent in the churches. They are not allowed to speak, but must be in submission, as the Law says. If they want to enquire about something, they should ask their own husbands at home; for it is disgraceful for a woman to speak in the church.

Did the word of God originate with you? Or are you the only people it has reached? If anybody thinks he is a prophet or spiritually gifted, let him acknowledge that what I am writing to you is the Lord's command. If he ignores this, he himself will be ignored.

Therefore, my brothers, be eager to prophesy, and do not forbid speaking in tongues. But everything should be done in a fitting and orderly way. (1 Cor. 14)

Once upon a time, long, long ago there were three missionaries in Japan and each one of them was used by God to plant a church. To this day you can still identify which of the three groups Christians come

101

from because each has its own distinctive way of praying. One group prays very quietly with great reverence: the whisperers. The second group prays with great fervour and very loudly as though they determine to make themselves heard in heaven itself: the ranters. The third group prays very moderately, not too loudly or too softly, but with peculiar hissing interjections: the whistlers. The first missionary had a very quiet voice, the second a very loud voice, and the third had teeth that did not fit! Their disciples had merely imitated their prayer styles.

Most people learn to participate in Christian activity, whether it is praying, preaching or worshipping, by imitating others rather than by following scriptural principles. Thus, as in the illustration above, they may copy something which is not significant at all, or which is a cultural hangover from someone's religious practice. The reference about clanging cymbals in Paul's comments about love is thought to refer to the pagan worship of the goddess Cybele. Thus 1 Corinthians 13:1 could be interpreted: 'If you do not have love, you might as well be participating still in the pagan worship of Cybele, the goddess of wild animals, amidst the clamour of clashing cymbals.' In some churches in Sarawak, one still notes confusion between noise and spirituality: some people compete with others to see who can pray loudest and longest. One suspects that this is a hangover from an older pagan tradition of worship.

The urge for instant replay

Christians in every part of the church are great imitators. But we must question whether this is the best way to learn. An evangelist once made a particular kind of appeal while a hymn was sung; or a relaxation technique before meditation was used; or individuals rose spontaneously to confess their sins; or unexpectedly individuals fell into a catatonic state; people held hands while healing was given; or in one instance supernatural knowledge of another's need was given. But then, by imitation, attempts have been made to repeat the event, or even to make it a regular feature of church activity. Something originally authentic given by the Lord, becomes instead a human methodology, a fossilized technique in a sincere attempt to recapture the first careless rapture! Sometimes it may even become a human attempt to manipulate God by means of some formula, to force him to repeat himself by reconstructing the earlier circumstances as exactly as possible.

Christians differ in their interpretation of Scripture. Some see the major biblical events as descriptive of a once-for-all unique action of God to be marvelled at, but not repeated. Others would see those same events as being prescriptive, and then attempt a replay of the action on a regular basis. Elijah experienced fire falling from heaven on Mount Carmel. It was a most effective demonstration of God's power. The human tendency would be to try to reproduce fire-falling on a regular basis. But when he went on to Mount Horeb, the Lord was 'not in the fire' this time, or even in the wind or the earthquake, but in the gentle whisper (1 Ki. 19:12). God is so rich in personality and creativity, that he is not bound to work in the same stereotyped way every time. He is able to do much more than we ask or imagine (Eph. 3:20), because his ways are much higher than our ways, and his thoughts than our thoughts (Is. 55:8–9). We can expect an infinite variety from our creative God.

Like Hercule Poirot, Agatha Christie's fictional detective, we are always wanting to make a reconstruction of earlier events. God is not a genie to be kept in a human bottle! We enjoy instant replays in cricket, boxing, tennis or football. We want to see it again.

When something in the spiritual realm impresses us, we want to see it again. 'Do it again, Lord, do it again!' we cry. So if we had our way, we would turn every unique sovereign intervention of God into the first of a long series. We read of events in Acts and assume that what we read must be prescriptive and repeatable, instead of descriptive of a unique and unrepeatable sovereign act of God. We endeavour to embalm every special event into our tradition. We attempt to take a sovereign act of God and make it into a technique of human manipulation.

For example, 'Full Gospel' groups now habitually use the word 'ministry' in a limited and unbiblical sense, to mean laying hands on people at the end of meetings so that they may be 'baptized in the Spirit', speak in tongues or receive healing: this then becomes a tradition, the only proper climax to a meeting. What was, when it first occurred, a genuine spontaneous event degenerates into an often repeated technique. It is as though we are afraid to let God be God – and imagine that he needs us to organize everything for him. We corrupt it all into a humanistic, man-centred Christianity.

It was reported in the Timor revival in Indonesia that water was miraculously turned into wine for them to use at a communion service. But then they started to pray every quarter for more water to be turned into wine on a regular basis. A team of earnest believers would pray for a week before each quarterly communion that the miracle would be repeated again and again. Perhaps it is not unspiritual to ask whether the Lord wants his people to spend a week in prayer for quarterly repetition of something that is reported as happening only once in Scripture (and then on a much more lavish scale!).

The difficulty of the replay tradition

Different groups of Christians develop different habits. They then become suspicious of traditions different from their own, and reluctant to accept them. And this in turn becomes a human barrier to fellowship and unity. In our example, from Japan, of the three ways of praying – all three groups are likely to regard their favoured way of praying as the best, and to look at other traditions with some suspicion and caution. Whisperers are prone to think the ranters immature and weak theologically. Ranters are likely to think whisperers both timid and deficient in faith. But some kind of compromise is possible: the ranters can come down a few decibels and the whisperers can be convinced that audibility is important, if the others are to join in with a true Amen. Each may still feel the others to be too loud or too muted: but how can you pray with the whistlers? No compromise seems possible, either you whistle or you don't! The same is true of other denominational gestures. Worshipping with hand-clappers can be quite deafening, as I discovered one day when standing next to vigorous Pentecostal friends.

I still remember with wry amusement watching my friend David Pawson on the platform of a New Zealand Baptist congregation which was split down the middle over charismatic issues. All waited to see whether he would identify with the arm-raisers or not. Would he half-raise both arms, or raise just one, or raise them in some verses and not others, or would he not raise them at all? The New Testament does certainly speak of men raising holy hands – but only on one single occasion (1 Tim. 2:8). We surely have the balance wrong in choruses where every other verse seems to call for this imitative behaviour. Is 'body language' not sometimes in danger of being that ostentation in worship that the Lord Jesus condemns as 'play-acting' (Mt. 6:2, 5)? It seems a pity when a fairly insignificant action is exalted to a sign of party membership.

Worship is not to be confined to a weekly corporate celebration

There has been an increasing tendency to speak of 'worship' in inverted commas, in parallel with a similar use of 'the gifts'. 'Will we use "the gifts" in chapel this morning?' asks an enthusiastic student. 'There seems little point in meeting at all unless we use gifts,' I reply. I am using the word in the sense it has held throughout church history, of all those gifts of verbal and nonverbal ministry described in Scripture. My friend with the silent inverted commas is using it in a more limited way, referring to a particular understanding of prophecy and tongues. In the same way, someone may comment that there was no 'worship' in chapel today, meaning that we only prayed, sang hymns and listened to God's Word without an extended period of singing choruses in a worshipful manner.

We must all applaud the greatly increased concern for genuine worship in recent years. To quote Terry Virgo:

A revolution has been taking place! Englishmen, as respectable as any invented, who formerly kept their hands battened resolutely as though they did not trust them out alone, have suddenly become hand-clapping, hand-raising enthusiasts!

Joyful praise and heartfelt worship have in many churches replaced the formal hymn singing which used to provide merely the prelude to the all-important preaching. 'Participation' has become the key word superseding passivity. Growing numbers of people are taking part in congregational worship with spoken and sung prophecies, tongues and interpretation, shared visions, or in playing musical instruments among growing church orchestras.

The manifestation of the presence of God has, on occasions, become almost breathtaking in its intensity, evoking sometimes shouts of joy and at other times tears of devoted adoration.[1]

The remainder of the article sensibly warns against thinking that such charismatic worship means 'singing recently written songs accompanied by guitars rather than old hymns accompanied by pipe organs'. It is stupid when, with a negative, conservative mindset, we reject what is good along with what is bad or merely peripheral. Reality in worship, and conscious, active, participation instead of mind-wandering, passive imitation, have to be an improvement. It is not fair to criticize the charismatic and renewal movements at their worst, any more than it is fair to assume that all more traditional services must, of necessity, be formal, dull and stereotyped.

The real issue is whether this is a biblical view of worship or not. Not only at weekly church meetings, but at Christian Union and other para-church meetings, it has become fashionable to start with a 'time of worship' – evoking joy instead of solemnity, informality rather than awe, celebration rather than stillness, though the best leaders make time for awed stillness as well. Not only is this regarded as an essential preparation of mind and heart for what is to follow, because our minds have been distracted by worldly cares, but, it is seen as being what God himself desires us to do. But is this assumption of the new orthodoxy correct?

Jewish singing of psalms was accompanied by musical instruments (the Greek word *psallō* originally meant to pluck or twang) and there is occasional mention of hand-clapping in the Psalms. But we must surely not assume that all biblical worship was restricted to the synagogue and temple services. If we limit 'worship' to a weekly rave-up we are only marginally better than the once-a-week formal church attenders, even if the reality and quality of what we do are higher.

In Scripture 'worship' is used in some remarkable contexts: for instance when Job lost all his property and his children, 'he fell to the ground in worship' (Jb. 1:20). It was solitary, and, far from being associated with a joyous spiritual 'high', it was agonizing misery. Job was acknowledging God's right to treat him to success or failure, blessing or disaster. Abraham's servant on the other hand was tired after a long journey, and had gone to the well to give the local talent the once-over. God had led him to a beautiful girl, courteous to an unknown foreigner (and kind to camels), who belonged to a God-fearing family: he bowed down and worshipped the Lord (Gn. 24:26). It was a solitary and genuine spontaneous outburst of gratitude, recorded for our benefit. Joshua, encamped before Jericho, challenged the warrior with the drawn sword. The warrior said, 'As commander of the army of the Lord, I have now come' (Jos. 5:10). Joshua fell down in worship. None of these were corporate or congregational experiences of worship, but human occasions of tragedy, thanksgiving or anxious anticipation.

Worship in Scripture then, is not something to be experienced only in celebration with the crowds journeying to Zion for festival, or in the temple courts at the offering of sacrifices. It is something which happens inwardly whenever a man or woman recognizes that God is sovereign and good, and rejoices in knowing such a God and being known by him. The writer of Deuteronomy spoke of this when he wrote:

Talk about them when you sit at home and when you walk along the road, when you lie down and when you get up . . . . (Dt. 6:7–8)

Thomas Haweis (1732–1820) wrote about the central place of worship in his hymn:

Fill Thou my life, O Lord my God,
    In every part with praise,
That my whole being may proclaim
    Thy being and Thy ways.

Not for the lip of praise alone,
    Nor e'en the praising heart,
I ask, but for a life made up
    Of praise in every part.

Praise in the common things of life,
    Its goings out and in;
Praise in each duty and each deed,
    However small and mean.

Fill every part of me with praise:
    Let all my being speak
Of Thee and of Thy love, O Lord,
    Poor though I be and weak.

So shall no part of day or night
    From sacredness be free;
But all my life in every step,
    Be fellowship with Thee.

Emil Brunner, writing about worship, says:

Yet it would be incorrect to say of the Ecclesia that it became real only in the act of assembly . . . for the first Christians were conscious of their membership of the Ecclesia even when the latter was not assembled for the cult. They understood their life to be a continuous act of worship apart from the cult altogether, when each individual in his particular walk of life, in the everyday world, in the family circle, or in his daily avocation, offered his life to Christ his Master as a sacrifice, well pleasing to God.[2]

Do Christians meet primarily to worship?

The answer is, almost certainly, *No*, not according to the Bible. The tendency to learn by imitation and assimilation from one's Christian subculture, rather than studying the Bible to discover the truth, is nowhere more evident than in the widespread assumption that the chief reason the church gathers together is for 'worship'. I freely admit that I also would have said so until relatively recently. But a London Bible College student writing an essay on worship drew my attention to an article by Howard Marshall, which questions that idea.

> A fundamental shift is called for. . . . While it is true in the broad sense that everything which the Christian does will be ultimately directed to the glory of God, it is simply not the case that the purpose of Christian meetings was understood as being primarily and directly worship, homage and adoration addressed to God.[3]

I find that I now agree with this insight, and am seeking to make this shift in my thinking and practice. In almost all traditions we have assumed that Christians meet for 'services of worship' and indeed in recent years, para-church groups also have begun to imagine that their meetings too must begin with 'worship'.

Marshall is not the only writer to advance such an opinion. Robert Banks, associated with house fellowships in Australia also writes;

> One of the most puzzling features of Paul's understanding of *ekklēsia* for his contemporaries, whether Jews or Gentiles, must have been his failure to say that a person went to church primarily to 'worship'. Not once in all his writing does he suggest this is the case. Indeed it could not be, for he held a view of 'worship' that prevented him from doing so.[4]

He then explains that since 'worship involves the whole of one's life, every word and action, and knows no special place or time' so that all times and places have now become the venue for worship, Paul cannot speak of Christians assembling together in church distinctively for this purpose. 'They are already worshipping God ... in whatever they are doing.' It is, therefore, not worship, but something else that marks off their coming together from everything else they are doing.[5] And that, Banks suggests, is the edification of their members through their God-given ministry to one another.

Marshall carefully analyses each of the 'worship' words used in the New Testament, because Christian practice needs to conform more closely to the Scriptures than it does at present. The vocabulary of worship, he argues, is used remarkably infrequently in descriptions of Christian meetings in the New Testament.

The word for priestly service (*leitourgeō*, from which the word 'liturgy' is derived in English) is used about Jewish priests, of giving aid to Christians (Rom. 15:27; Phil. 2:25, 30) and only in one instance to a church meeting, and then not of a congregation but only of its leaders meeting together in Antioch (Acts 13:2).

111

The second word group used for the reverence that people show to God (*sebomai*) is used only once of what happens when Christians meet together, and not by them about themselves, but by Jews criticizing Paul for persuading people to worship in ways contrary to the Law (Acts 18:13).

A third word group (*latreuō*) used of Jewish worship, and in the book of Revelation is 'not applied specifically to Christian meetings in such a way as to sum up what was taking place'.

A fourth word group (*proskyneō*) used of the apostles worshipping Jesus when they met him risen from the dead, is used only once of what happens at a Christian meeting, not of what the Christians themselves do but of the 'outsider' (1 Cor. 14:25).

Marshall sums up his whole significant examination by saying:

> Although the whole activity of Christians can be described as the service of God and they are engaged throughout their lives in worshipping him, yet this vocabulary is not applied in any specific way to Christian meetings . . . the remarkable fact is that Christian meetings are not said to take place specifically in order to worship God and the language of worship is not used as a means of referring to them or describing them.[6]

The apostles' doctrine, fellowship, breaking of bread and prayers

The contemporary emphasis on the primacy of worship is often, contrary to what is frequently claimed, *man-centred*. Services and meetings which

112

begin with 'worship' that is an offering from man to God, have put the cart before the horse. If we are truly God-centred then we must begin with a movement from God to man, a movement of grace.

After Pentecost the description of Christian activity in Acts 2:42 does not specifically include worship as one of their activities at all but the succession of ideas puts what man offers to God *last* rather than first.

a. The apostles' teaching

It is mentioned first that the initial movement is from God to man. And this seems to correspond with that area of teaching ministry concerning which Paul instructed Timothy, 'Until I come, devote yourself to the public reading of Scripture, to preaching and to teaching' (1 Tim. 4:13). It is unfortunate that the NIV translates this verse as 'to preaching and to teaching' rather than 'the exhortation and the teaching' (*te paraklēsei, te didaskalia*). The 'exhortation' is the same word used in Acts 13:15 for the exposition that followed the reading of the Law and the Prophets in the synagogue. The 'teaching' was perhaps a word for teaching drawn more widely from the whole of Scripture, and it was to be Timothy's work. Thus it seems that the primary reason for the churches coming together in the New Testament was in order to hear the Word of God and obey it (Lk. 8:21; 11:28); and this identified them as the new family of Jesus.

The concept of upbuilding or 'edification', as it used to be called, seems strongest at this point, as in 1 Corinthians 14:5, 12, 26 and Ephesians 4:12 where the building up of the church, or the body of Christ, is seen as the *supreme* purpose of spiritual gifts and of the church coming together.

> ... these meetings of worship had precisely the dominating purpose of building up the Body of Christ. The assemblies were edifying, not in our

113

colourless sense of the word, but in the strict and literal sense of building up.[7]

In connection with the visits of the Lord Jesus to the synagogue, rather than 'worship' it is the word 'teaching' which stands out again and again (Mt. 4:23; Mk. 1:21; 6:2; Lk. 4:15; 6:6; 13:10; Jn. 6:59; 18:20).

b. Fellowship

The second movement is from man to man. The word 'fellowship' carries the idea of 'sharing' or even of being business partners (Lk. 5:10). So the idea of helping others materially is included, and elaborated in Acts 2:45 where 'they gave to anyone as he had need'. In Romans 15:26 the same word is used for 'contribution for the poor among the saints in Jerusalem' and also in the following verse for 'sharing' in spiritual blessings. The effect of the Lord ministering to us through his Word is that we are moved to minister to one another. Reconciliation with God in Christ, should also cause us to be reconciled with our brothers and sisters. We are to lift up holy hands in prayer 'without anger and disputing'.

Spiritual gifts are not only verbal, speaking gifts like teaching, prophesying and exhorting, used in the first movement, but also they may be non-verbal – serving, contributing to the needs of others, showing mercy (Rom. 12:7–8), helping others (1 Cor. 12:28). This is a second reason why Christians come together: in order to minister to each others' needs. Brunner says it was not only the act of meeting in itself that was important but its character – aimed at making out of the mere assembly an act of vital co-operation.[8]

c. Breaking of bread

Here again there is the downward movement of God's grace. There is no altar but the cross. God has acted. The bread and the wine are the emblems of Christ's broken body and shed blood. Yet at the same time that

114

'sharing' (1 Cor. 10:16–17) is also seen as an expression that we are all united in 'one loaf', so the horizontal dimension is there also. Many Protestant traditions see the breaking of bread as central to the meeting of the church: Anglo-Catholic and Christian Brethren, for example. God is at work to bless the participants with his grace, and at the same time he unites us with one another.

d. Prayers

Finally we come to movement from man to God, but it is spoken of after the movements from God to man, and not before it. Now that God has spoken, revealed his will, reminded us of his promises, and especially of his provision for us in Christ, we are to respond by praying. First, he has ministered to us, and we have ministered to one another. How can we not respond? What shall I render to the Lord for all his benefits towards me (Ps. 116:12)? So there certainly is a responsive movement from us to him, which must include prayer and thanksgiving. 1 Timothy 2:1–2, 8 suggests that such prayer was a regular part of Christian gathering. But this response of man to God is one which emphasizes man's dependance upon God. The word 'worship', however, is not included at all.

The work of deacons and elders and spiritual gifts

No list of spiritual gifts in the New Testament includes the gift of 'leading worship', which suggests that whatever the contemporary trend, this was not seen as significant in the New Testament churches.

Another interesting and confirming piece of evidence is that the various descriptions of qualifications for Christian workers do not seem to give any priority to leading worship. The descriptions in the Pastoral Epistles are more character requirements than job descriptions, and therefore the very brevity of descriptions of their work are all the more significant.

The overseer (bishop) . . . must be able to teach (1 Tim. 3:2).
Deacons . . . must keep hold of the deep truths of the faith (1 Tim. 3:9).
The elders who direct the affairs of the church well . . . especially those whose work is preaching and teaching (1 Tim. 5:17).
. . . entrust to reliable men who will be able to teach . . . (2 Tim. 2:2).
An overseer . . . must hold firmly to the trustworthy message . . . so that he can encourage others with sound doctrine (Tit. 1:9).

What is true of 'worship' words in the New Testament, *i.e.* that they are not used in connection with Christian meetings, also seems to be true of Christian workers: they are not described in relation to worship either!

The influence of the synagogue

In an interesting recording of a service from St Andrew's Church in Chorleywood, the speaker made the fascinating comment that it seemed very difficult to find out much about worship from the New Testament: 'There is no model . . . we cannot find out what actually happened. Their model was the Old Testament . . .'. He then went on, wrongly in my view, to find his model in the worship of the pre-exilic temple! However, as Howard Marshall points out:

It follows that the nearest contemporary analogy to the church meeting was provided by the synagogue, and not by the temple.[9]

116

Jesus and the apostles grew up in a cultural environment dominated by the synagogue. True, they went up to the Jerusalem temple for the great feasts, but for most of the year it was the synagogue that was the focus of their worship of the one true God: and it was therefore only natural that the synagogue pattern of 'worship' should have the greatest influence upon the shape of Christian meeting. The chief purpose of the synagogue was that the Torah was read and taught, heard and learned there. It was a place of instruction and prayer.[10]

There are no less than fifty-seven references to the synagogue in the New Testament. In the gospels Jesus and his disciples are found in the synagogue many times and in Acts Paul always seems to have made a bee-line for the synagogue, if there was one, in every new city that he visited.

Jesus himself 'on the sabbath day ... went into the synagogue, as was his custom' (Lk. 4:16). In Galilee his ministry began in the synagogues. Responding to the High Priest's questioning, Jesus replied, 'I always taught in the synagogues or at the temple, where all the Jews came together' (Jn. 18:20).

As Galileans, the Lord Jesus and a number of the apostles would have been in the synagogue sabbath by sabbath, visiting the Jerusalem temple only for the great annual festivals. The pattern of synagogue worship would have been most influential, and we know that both the Law and the prophets were read there (Acts 13:15, 27; 15:21). The reading was followed by an exhortation based upon it (Acts 13:15; Lk. 4:21–23). When Paul wrote to Timothy about his ministry (1 Tim. 4:13), he told him that until Paul comes he was to devote himself to 'the public reading of Scripture', to (literally) 'the exhortation' (same word as Acts 13:15) and finally 'to the teaching'.

This certainly suggests that that same centrality of the reading and exposition of the Law and the

117

Prophets in the synagogue was continued in the churches of Christ. We should also bear in mind that the Psalms were sung in the synagogue, and that these do express a responsive movement from man to God in praise and worship. But it cannot be denied that it was the movement from God to man that was central in the reading of the divinely given Law, and the messages that came from God to the prophets. Though the Psalms were originally a human response to God, they too are part of the God-given Scriptures, so that even when we worship we use words given by God himself.

We should remember that the temple was not only a place for the offering of sacrifices. It was also a place for teaching (Lk. 2:46; 19:47; 20:1; Jn. 18:20), for giving of alms (Lk. 21:1), for the healing ministry (Lk. 5:14, of the leper, *etc.*) and for rejoicing and feasting in the presence of the Lord (Dt. 14:25–26). So, while the synagogue would have been more influential because the Lord and the apostles would have been present there every sabbath to hear the Law and the Prophets read, the temple in Jerusalem was the centre for much more than the cultus, the offering of sacrifices and 'services of worship'.

1 Timothy 4:13 seems to have been disregarded by those who have thought that 1 Corinthians 14:26–33 is the only biblical prescription of which elements should be included in a Christian gathering. But that description also includes singing psalms, teaching, a revelation, a tongue, an interpretation (and in the synagogue the reading of the Scriptures in classical Hebrew had to be interpreted into vernacular speech). Verses 29–31 seem to identify prophecy with giving a revelation, and then the purpose of their prophesying is said to be 'so that all may be instructed and encouraged' (verse 31), which again seems to identify it with the exhortation and teaching of 1 Timothy 4:13.

The building up of the church

The overall purpose for meeting together given in 1 Corinthians 14:26 is for the strengthening of the church (literally, for building up or edification). This bears out what both Banks and Marshall have said; that listening to God speak through the Scriptures and mutual upbuilding of one another by sound teaching were the primary reasons for meeting.

Ephesians gives us further clues in that the gifts given by the ascended Christ are 'to equip God's people for works of service, so that the body of Christ may be built up' (4:12). The filling of the whole congregation with the Spirit ('you all go on being filled . . .') is seen to have four consequences (Eph. 5:18–21):

speaking to one another with psalms, hymns and spiritual songs;
singing and making music in your hearts to the Lord;
always giving thanks to God the Father for everything;
submitting to one another out of reverence for Christ.

At first sight this seems to place less emphasis on teaching. But it does not talk of speaking to God first, but rather of speaking to one another. If it is true that Ephesians and Colossians were written at the same time and sent by the same messenger Tychichus (Eph. 6:21; Col. 4:7), then we can get further light by comparing it with the similar section in Colossians 3:16:

Let the word of Christ dwell in you richly as you teach and admonish one another with all wisdom, and as you sing psalms, hymns and spiritual songs with gratitude in your hearts to God.

It really does seem that we need a definite shift in our emphases, even though this will not be popular in traditional churches which have always spoken of their services as 'divine worship', or in charismatic churches which have felt that worship was meant to be primary.

> It is simply not the case that the purpose of Christian meetings was understood as being primarily and directly worship, homage and adoration addressed to God ... consequently, *it is a mistake* to regard the main or indeed the only purpose of Christian meetings as being the worship of God, a view which leads to their structure being determined in terms of what we offer to God in and through Christ.[11]

Marshall insists that 'the primary element is the God-man movement, downward rather than upward, in which God comes to his people and uses his human servants to convey his salvation to them, to strengthen and upbuild them.' It is here that listening to God's Word is important. The stress on 'worship' in recent years has meant that all our meetings have to start with an extended period of chorus singing (which may or may not be identifiable as worship). Yet this is beginning with man, rather than God: with works rather than grace. Pagan worship often does begin with people calling on gods to come down into their meeting, and hoping that they will condescend to come. Our God is not like that.

A Christian meeting is different. God is already present. He always is present (1 Cor. 14:25 'God is really among you'; Mt. 18:20 'there I am with them'). We do not have to call him to join us. The initiative always comes from him, the eager outgoing God. He does not have to be persuaded by us, or ministered to by us, as though he needed our worship. He pours his grace upon reluctant men and women through his Word. *Our* response is secondary, not his! It may be said that our subjective feelings mean that we do not recognize his presence, and need therefore to draw near to God in our own consciousness, knowing that he will draw near to us.

Yes, there should be a man-to-God movement in worship, but this must be seen as secondary, as human response to divine grace. During the period of David Pawson's ministry at Millmead in Guildford, we often began with the ministry of the Word, and worship was somehow much more real *after* we had listened to the Word of God. Ministry by God to us must be primary: worship is our response to his grace. But as prayer and worship are also 'in the Spirit', that is by means of the Spirit as the channel, God is at work even in our responding (Eph. 2:18).

There will also be a man-to-man movement, as we seek to build one another up mutually; and indeed as God-given charismata are used both in speaking to and serving of one another, this ministry also may be seen as inspired and sustained by the flow of God's grace.

So when Christians meet it is emphatically *not* that we have to call God down, or 'build his throne' before we can do anything else. His throne endures from the beginning to the end, and owes nothing to our feeble endeavours. He is always present and does not need to be called up, or his attention caught, as pagan worship so often does. We need to realize his presence afresh perhaps; we need to hear his authentic Word in Scripture rather than the sometimes banal lyrics of our human choruses, and with the help of his Spirit we shall both respond to him and be enabled to serve one another.

My colleague Ian McNair reminds me that a servant must first accept the instructions of his master, before he can properly serve at all. So we must first listen to our Master's word and only then can we respond.

Teaching and upbuilding are primary, so that proclamation of the Word followed by response to his word seems to be the proper pattern. Fellowship and mutual upbuilding are also important, and can happen only when the church meets. There seems little point in engaging in solitary exercises when gathered with others – this was one of Paul's arguments against speaking in 'tongues' (1 Cor. 14:9, 11–12) in meetings.

There is one other aspect of the contemporary emphasis on worship that is rather worrying. There is confusion between the euphoria that is generated by a large crowd all singing together in celebration, and worshipping in spirit and in truth. They are not necessarily the same thing: you can enjoy such human euphoria in other large crowds, perhaps at a football match, the Olympic Games, a concert with lots of audience participation, a crowd outside Buckingham Palace, or at a Nuremberg Hitler Youth Rally. What worries me is the feeling that we have to have chorus singing in order to generate 'worship', whereas what the 'song-leader' is generating may be no more than group euphoria. It helps if we are aware of the danger and do not mistake one for the other.

Conclusion

We need to give thought and prayer to our church meetings. The church does not exist only when we meet in plenary session. But our meetings provide opportunities to realize afresh our identity as a church of God, as the body of Christ, to affirm and encourage one another in our walk as believers, and to express our solidarity with one another and our union with the Lord.

Our chief reason for meeting may be mutual upbuilding, but we shall want to worship when we come together because it is something we should be doing 'at all times'. It is fitting that we do praise God together on our knees, that we lift up our hearts to him, and (if it helps us) our hands as well.

Thus, while agreeing with Marshall that, if we are to be biblical, we need 'a shift' away from seeing worship as the main reason for assembling, worship will still remain one of the significant things that happens, as we respond to God revealing himself to us through his Word. We shall not meet primarily in order to worship, nor feel that we must first work up a feeling of worship, but as we realize afresh what God is like, and what he has done, there ought to be a fresh, spontaneous and joyful response in worship.

THE MISSION OF THE CHURCH

What on earth is it for?

Then Jesus came to them and said, 'All authority in heaven and on earth has been given to me. Therefore go and make disciples of all nations, baptising them in the name of the Father and of the Son and of the Holy Spirit, and teaching them to obey everything I have commanded you. And surely I am with you always, to the very end of the age.' (Mt. 28:18–20)

'You have heard that it was said, "Love your neighbour and hate your enemy." But I tell you: Love your enemies and pray for those who persecute you, that you may be sons of your Father in heaven. He causes his sun to rise on the evil and the good, and sends rain on the righteous and the unrighteous. If you love those who love you, what reward will you get? Are not even the tax collectors doing that? And if you greet only your brothers, what are you doing more than others? Do not even pagans do that? Be perfect, therefore, as your heavenly Father is perfect . . .' (Mt. 5:43–18)

When the crowds heard this, they were astonished at his teaching.

Hearing that Jesus had silenced the Sadducees, the Pharisees got together. One of them, an expert in the law, tested him with this question: 'Teacher, which is the greatest commandment in the Law?'

> *Jesus replied: '"Love the Lord your God with all your heart and with all your soul and with all your mind." This is the first and greatest commandment. And the second is like it: "Love your neighbour as yourself." All the Law and the Prophets hang on these two commandments.'* (Mt. 22:34–40)

To me, as a former missionary to Japan, the familiar words of the 'Great Commission' come home with particular force. This is because in Japanese culture the moment of departure is regarded as having great significance. So too is the obligation to obey to the letter and to the death the words of one's liege lord. Even if the impact of parting words is less in European cultures, and loyalty to lords is not absolute, we have to affirm that Jesus' last words before leaving this earth and ascending to his Father must carry great weight.

> Therefore go and make disciples of all nations, baptising them in the name of the Father and of the Son and of the Holy Spirit, and teaching them to obey everything I have commanded you (Mt. 28:19–20).

Luke wrote some equally significant words in Acts, where Jesus says:

> . . . you will be my witnesses in Jerusalem, and in all Judea and Samaria, and to the ends of the earth (Acts 1:8).

The fact that the first passage needs to be read in the light of Daniel 7:14 and the second in the light of Isaiah 43:6–12 increases the huge impact of Jesus' power and authority in commanding his servants.

The implications for the baptized disciple are considerable. For us, being Christians means we must belong to our Master's church and also be totally committed to his cause. He has constituted his church to be a worldwide evangelization society! If we are to remain faithful to the commands of the Lord Jesus Christ, we must evangelize everyone, whatever their existing religious convictions, however intolerant and contrary to the spirit of a 'multi-faith society' that may seem. Muslims equally dedicated to the growth of Islam understand this commitment of ours.

This responsibility will be fulfilled in two main ways – locally, within the parish or effective area of direct outreach from the local church, and universally, in ever-widening circles as each congregation reaches out from its own 'Jerusalem' to its own Judea, Samaria and to the ends of the earth. It is fatal to dichotomize these two things. The church which is deeply engaged in evangelism in its own neighbourhood will have members with evangelistic gifts, readily transferable to other churches in other cultures. It will not only believe that non-Christians can be converted, but have direct experience of it happening, and therefore a much greater expectation of it continuing to happen. It is all one world and countries overseas are 'merely an accident of Continental drift'.

Are we just playing at soldiers?

When I am asked to speak to some congregations from Ephesians 6, I face several problems: one is that they think they already know all about this passage and its teaching, and the other is my own sense of the ludicrous, for to think of certain congregations as 'marching to war' is pure fantasy! The whole thing has a disturbing Walter Mitty flavour! (James Thurber wrote an amusing little piece called *The Secret Life of Walter Mitty* – immortalized by Danny Kaye in a film of the same name about a husband wheeling a trolley around the supermarket while his wife shops and who fantasizes in a whole series of heroic daydreams with himself cast in the leading role.)

Now it is easy at this point for us to engage in a 'cop out' and to think that this may be true of many wishy-washy liberal congregations, but cannot be true of a well-known evangelical congregation like ours. But unfortunately I pick up this sense of unreality in famous evangelical congregations too! It is evangelicals who accept the need to evangelize, and this means that if evangelism is ineffective then we as evangelicals are failing to reach non-Christians.

We may be less to blame than other Christians for failure to evangelize, but by the same test we must be more to blame for failure *in* evangelism.[1]

A scrutiny of the church growth figures provided by Peter Brierley in the *UK Christian Handbook*[2] shows that over the twenty-year period from 1970 to 1990 Anglicans will have lost more than 25% of their membership, like the Presbyterians. The Methodists will have lost more than 30%, and the Baptists 22%. More than four million nominal church members (included in these figures) attend church less than once a month, and there are forty million non-Christians, who are hardly ever in a church, unreached by the British church 'army'! The mainline churches are decreasing at a rate of 2.5% per annum. This is in no way offset by the increasing membership of 'house churches' which are calculated at having around 120,000 members, equivalent only to around two and a half years' loss of Anglican membership. The purpose of these figures is not to arouse pessimism and defeatism, but to wake us up from our Walter Mitty fantasies of, 'like a mighty army moves the church of God', to the reality of the spiritual battle ahead of us. We need to waken up if we are to evangelize the 91% English, 87% Welsh and 83% Scots people who are outside of the churches.

We cannot win that spiritual battle by singing happily to each other and to the Lord safely inside our evangelical bunkers, deploring the lamentable state of the world outside. The evangelistic rallies of the late 40s and 50s seem to have been replaced by the celebration events of the 80s, as though we are happier talking to one another than communicating with the pagan world.

Jo Bayley in his book *The Gospel Blimp*[3] caricatures Christians as being so hectically busy in their church activities and organizations that they are failing to reach their next-door neighbours with the gospel. There is more activity, more newly formed Christian societies being registered as charities than ever before, but there is less and less effectiveness in winning non-Christians. The biggest problem we face is how to end the 'phoney war' and get our churches to come out of our trenches and foxholes, to motivate one another to engage the enemy on his territory and take prisoners for the Lord.

Local church responsibility for evangelizing its neighbourhood

A local church is an advance position of the Lord's army which is expected to advance and take territory from the enemy, wearing the sure sandals of the gospel of peace and wielding the sword of the Spirit. A church does not justify its existence merely by existing, by occupying a building twice on Sundays and holding services.

The greatest problem of 'mission' is motivating a local congregation to evangelize its own immediate neighbourhood. How often have we all been exhorted from the pulpit to get on with it, and how infrequently does a congregation as a whole get the message and march out to do battle.

I am not talking about organizing 'a mission', which

129

is often a substitute for the real thing, particularly when a surrogate team of people from outside are invited in to do the work, while local people come along to see how well they are getting on with it! Why are Christians so slow to take the Great Commission seriously? If challenged with the need overseas, we murmur about the need in this country, but that is no more than a feeble excuse, if we then fail even to evangelize within our own neighbourhood.

Very many Christians seem content with the *status quo*. We feel frustrated by the lack of progress and the depressing statistics, and wish that 'someone' would do something about it, but congregations as a whole remain passive and inactive. That liberal churches with little understanding of the gospel should be like this is not surprising. The extraordinary tragedy is that evangelical, Bible-believing Christians who see the need for evangelism often, in fact, do no more than give lip service to it. So although we are responsible for all the evangelistic efforts that do take place, in effect we do little and consequently achieve little.

Some people are understandably very critical of mass evangelism in terms of its cost-effectiveness — all that time and money and so few lasting conversions. A good case can be made that evangelism centred on the local church and its regular work is more effective: but just recognizing this effectiveness is not the same as achieving it!

Some valid approaches

There have been some outstanding attempts to help us Christians out of our passivity, to get over our reserve and shyness, to make us more coherent and explicit in our witness. Everything is worth trying! Here are some useful resources.

Care to Say Something[4]
This is an excellent workbook, which can be used by small groups to get them praying for non-Christians whom they meet almost every day. They then pray for opportunities to witness to them naturally, and go on praying step by step. Our church studied this book together and I found it most helpful. It has a very popular style, with pictures and captions, discussion in pairs and groups, grids to fill in and so on. Excellent!

A Man's Life[5]
Two thirds of active church members are women. Women read more Christian books. Women's groups are active in most churches. Men's groups are less effective, and men returning from work are reluctant to go to mid-week activities. We are not effective in evangelizing men. *A Man's Life* is aimed at correcting this imbalance, and again is a popular workbook with video clips available. It is well worth trying.

Good News Down the Street[6]
This is a modified form of *Evangelism Explosion* adapted for reserved British people. It is based upon persuading people contacted at baptisms, weddings and funerals, as well as those met through door-to-door visiting who showed special interest, to invite a small team of local Christians to come to their home and explain their faith in a brief series. It is very non-threatening and can be terminated by them at any point. The original scheme used the course with two hundred individuals (including sixty-three couples) over a six-year period. Eighty nine teams were sent out involving one hundred and twenty different members of the congregation. Of one hundred and fifty contacted in this way five failed to complete the course; fifteen were already Christians; one hundred and thirty six made a commitment to Christ; four have made a commitment since; forty made no positive decision. Not much evangelism achieves a

131

70% success rate, doubling the number of Christians in a six-year period. We would all be pleased if we saw that happening in our congregations.

Of course, situations vary. The parent congregation of Christian Brethren in Singapore in recent years has seen 80% of its membership baptized as adults over a five year period. This may provoke us to incredulity (and envy perhaps), but the Lord is the same there as here. The limitations are put there by us and the society in which we live.

Know and Tell the Gospel[7]
This is a very practical and helpful book by a gifted Australian evangelist from the diocese of Sydney, written in an easy to read, down-to-earth style. Motivation is nine-tenths of success, and people develop their own methods as their experience of evangelizing grows.

The link between local evangelism and world mission

There is no doubt that churches which are active in evangelism and soul-winning in their own locality also produce good missionaries. Those churches which never see conversions just do not produce the evangelists and church-planters who are so desperately needed around the world. But those people whose appetite has been whetted by being involved in fruitful work in which they see the impact of the gospel upon individuals and families find this so satisfying that they want to give their whole lives to the proclamation of the gospel and the building up of disciples. Churches in which conversions are a weekly occurrence become training grounds, continually turning out full-time Christian workers, ministers and missionaries. They are very closely linked together, so that wherever you find one you find the other. Ghetto churches, self-absorbed with their own in-groups, fail both in local outreach and in missionary vision: the disease causes lack of fruit both locally and in the wider world.

Historically many missionary societies were founded as the product of a time of spiritual quickening and accelerated church growth. Today it is the revitalized, growing church which produces most missionaries.

Local church responsibilty for worldwide mission

The obligation of every baptized disciple to obey Christ's commands, not least the final command to make disciples of all nations, means that concern for mission is not to be confined to the super-keen, lunatic fringe of the congregation who make time to attend extra prayer meetings. There has been increasing concern to educate the churches, expressed in such books as *Ten Sending Churches*.[8]

But at the same time, many churches seem to have been diverted from a clear understanding of mission and its chief aims. The 'Acts' of the apostles were principally evangelistic journeys, with the result that men and women were saved, baptized and integrated into local churches. I still believe this to be the chief task of mission today. The ministries of healing and social concern were not an end in themselves for the apostles, but were associated with a primary thrust in evangelism, training disciples and building them together into new churches.

At the beginning of what the church historian Kenneth Latourette called the 'great century' – the nineteenth – there were virtually no Protestant churches in the three great continents of Latin America, Africa and Asia. There were no American missionary societies until 1810, and it was only in the closing years of the eighteenth century that British missionary societies were first founded: the Baptist Missionary Society in 1792, the London Missionary Society in 1793, and the Church Missionary Society in 1799. Carey had only recently settled in Serampore in India, while Morrison did not reach Canton till 1807. Judson landed in Burma in 1813, the same year that the first missionaries to the Javanese landed in Batavia and the year that David Livingstone was born. Despite the missionaries' short life expectancy there were growing churches almost everywhere by the end of the century. It is true that cities like Singapore and Sydney did not even exist at that time and countries like Vietnam, Laos, Cambodia, Nepal, Tibet and Afghanistan had to wait for the twentieth century. But in view of poor medical treatment, slow sea travel and short life expectancy, the extent of the missionary work of the nineteenth century was a truly remarkable achievement.

The twentieth century saw a noticeable shift of emphasis. Once the task of church-planting had been started, what further need was there for missionaries? The apostolic pattern seeems to have been lost: the theory was that national churches would now take over and evangelize their own fellow-countrymen. But in many cases they failed to do so, often because the boundaries of nations were the artificial legacy of colonialism, and there were ethnic and cultural boundaries within 'nations' that were very difficult to cross. In Pakistan, for example, 95% of Christians come from a Hindu background and are ill-equipped to reach their Muslim fellow-countrymen.

One effect of this is that the older denominational missions moved increasingly into much-appreciated institutions like schools and hospitals. These assisted colonial development, but were not effective evangelistically, except possibly in countries very resistant to the gospel where prejudice had to be overcome and confidence established.

The recently initiated Church Growth movement was started by a man called Donald McGavran who had already retired from missionary service in India. What he was attempting to do was to draw the attention of these older denominational missions to their loss of effectiveness in evangelism and church-planting, and to call them back to 'the saving of souls, baptizing of bodies and planting of churches'. Fortunately the wave of 'Inland Missions' that began with Hudson Taylor's China Inland Mission in 1865, and continued in the post World War II American G.I. missions have largely kept their goals of evangelism and church-planting clear, and have been more influenced by McGavran than the older denominational missions were.

Number of missionaries per 10,000 denominational members[9]

Brethren 88	Anglican 11
Baptist 61	Methodist 6
Pentecostal 36	Presbyterian 3
Salvation Army 34	

The latter part of the twentieth century also saw a great diminution of long-term missionaries from Britain and even more from other European countries, only partially offset by the beginning of the so-called 'Third World' missions. The post-war 50s had produced large numbers of committed long-term missionaries, but by the 80s it seems that fewer young people are willing to face the financial implications. In the nineteenth century they were not bothered about whether they would be able to maintain their professional standing or afford to buy retirement housing – less than half survived the first term of service anyway, in the early years of work in West Africa and Thailand.

This change in attitude has meant that young people who feel some commitment, volunteer for short-term service in large numbers. But they have little time to learn the language or to appreciate the necessity of adapting to cultural context. They constitute a force of youthful, enthusiastic but inexperienced amateurs who can speak only their own European languages. Some may be naïvely enthusiastic for signs and wonders as a short-cut to evangelism (apparently unknown to their 'unspiritual' predecessors, who were willing to give their lifelong energies to learning language and loving people). This is, admittedly, the most odious of comparisons, but one can only wish that young people today were prepared to give the long-term commitment that their grandparents did.

Church-perfecting

Once national churches have been planted, missionary groups must not impede or retard the speedy development of national leaders, especially in fresh evangelism and church-planting. Sadly, national leadership can sometimes get rusted up in the nuts and bolts of church organization and politics, and consequently outreach slows down. The table at the end of this chapter shows the variety of work in which expatriates can still be involved under national leadership. A strong national church which has penetrated every stratum of society (*e.g.* Kenya or Korea) needs fewer international fellow-workers than a smaller national church which has an established bridgehead but is confined within certain social or ethnic communities.

At every stage it is essential not only that the missionary works under national leadership, but that there are also national trainees, who will in due course replace the expatriate. The church-planting missionary in a given locality seeks to be replaced by a local Christian who will take over the leadership. This does not mean that the missionary therefore leaves the country; he merely moves to a new pioneer area and starts all over again. In a responsive field, it is to be hoped that any church-planting missionary is able to move on after four or five years having planted a church under national leadership, and encouraged them to go on planting daughter churches.

Or let us suppose that there is only one theological college for the training of full-time workers, and this is initially staffed and led by expatriates. The goal must be to appoint a national principal as soon as a suitably trained person becomes available, while recognizing that some continuing expatriate involvement in teaching may be advisable on a steadily reducing basis. The retiring expatriate principal, however, will usually need to move out of the situation, though humble people have sometimes been able to carry on in a subsidiary, supporting role when they have posed no threat to their national successors.

Working in a variety of church-related ministries under national church leadership demands humility and almost a different personality type from the 'strong, natural leader' image of the pioneer church-planter: there is a place here for gentle, self-effacing, tactful missionaries, who always esteem the national Christian better than themselves (Phil. 2:3). A wide range of work is still necessary, after the pioneer church-planting phase under expatriate missionary leadership has been completed.

Priorities in mission

Individuals have to decide their own priorities in terms of the gifts which God has given them, and their sense of calling. If they do not they will be carried about by every wind, trying a bit of this and a bit of that, and end up without having achieved anything worthwhile in terms of a life-work. There is never any problem in finding things to do, and a missionary's time can always be filled to overflowing; but there must be a clear policy established by missionary societies (and sometimes there is not!) and by the individual in recognizing priorities.

Missionary societies also have to establish their priorities and policies in line with their history, opportunities and calling. They are especially in danger when they have responsibly passed over leadership to national churches, because they can respond to a variety of *ad hoc* needs without any clear policy and end up as a 'mission of the gaps' that continues to recruit candidates, but which lacks clear field goals. This has been an especial problem for denominational societies.

Local churches also can respond in a higgledy-piggledy kind of way to immediate interests of some new arrival, but without formulating any clear policies or having any clear sense of direction. Let me indicate some crucial areas where priorities have to be faced.

a. Overseas or home

The recognition that there are needs in the home country is anything but a new insight, and I was amused to discover that William Carey wrote powerfully against this argument 190 years ago!

It has been objected that there are multitudes in our own nation, and within our immediate spheres of action, who are as ignorant as the South-Sea savages, and that therefore we have work enough at home, without going into other countries. That there are thousands in our own land as far from God as possible, I readily grant, and that this ought to excite us to ten-fold diligence in our work, and in attempts to spread divine knowledge amongst them is a certain fact; but that it ought to supersede all attempts to spread the gospel in foreign parts seems to want proof. Our own countrymen have the means of grace and may attend the word preached if they chuse it . . .[10]

138

In terms of relative needs, the table below, showing the ratio of Christian workers to human population (not to Christians), demonstrates the great imbalance that exists. It is much easier to find a Christian worker in Europe and the United States than in the rest of the world.

Within Africa the figures would be very different when we realize that Christian workers are almost non-existent in North African countries, and much fewer in francophone Africa compared with English speaking African countries. Consequently there is a ratio in English-speaking Africa much closer to that in North America. Within the European scene there would be a much lower number of Christian workers in Latin Europe than in Germany or Britain. While there certainly is a need for Christian workers in Britain, it is frankly rubbish to say that the need is greater than it is in Asia, for example. Evangelical Anglicans in particular, with their longstanding interest in East Africa, are prone to extrapolate from those strong and revived churches, with their minimal need for missionaries, to the rest of the world. They are in danger of concluding that the need for missionaries is almost over. But that is not true in many other parts of Africa, let alone in neglected Asia.

Continent	Population 1970	Christian workers	People per worker
N. America	226 million	776,749	291
Europe	459 million	1,059,742	433
Africa	356 million	431,321	816
S. America	283 million	257,312	1,100
South Asia	1,101 million	235,102	4,685
East Asia	926 million	46,319	20,000

(Figures are from Peter Cotterell after Overseas Crusades)

b. *Frontline or ancillary*

Ask some churches what missionaries they have sent out, and you may be told that they have a short-termer, a Bible translator, someone in relief work or someone in radio work. Mischievously, to make my point (and not because I disregard their present contribution or denigrate their work), I reply 'Hm! No real missionaries, then!'

I do this because I want them to think about priorities! Yet this pattern can be found in church after church, and it is having a deleterious effect in many countries. Someone from Pakistan recently commented to me that of 400 missionaries in that country only ten were in direct evangelism and church-planting (though many other fine Christians are witnessing in the course of medical and other Christian work).

Ephesians 6 tells us about the armour of God. We are God's army. The Roman Empire of Paul's day needed legions of fighting troops as well as auxiliaries. Standard-makers, horn-blowers, armourers, farriers, and surgeons were all essential to those ancient armies, but the Empire would never have expanded as it did without the legions of frontline fighters.

The modern missionary force is very lopsided: you cannot win a battle with Signals, Catering Corps, the Army Dental Corps, and a group of dispatch-riders and dog-handlers! You must have infantry, marines, paratroops and assault regiments in order to win a war. Please do not misunderstand me: I do not want fewer medical and relief workers. I want more evangelists and church-planters. They are absolutely vital if we are to reverse the falling percentage of Christians.

Part of the problem is the glamour of so-called 'specialized work'. Flying aeroplanes, broadcasting, or translating sounds more professional than just preaching the gospel! And the obsession that people have for using their training means that they think more about using their technical skills than about preaching and teaching. The gospel would never have got beyond Galilee if the apostles had insisted on finding some way of continuing as fishermen or tax collectors.

As a child I was fascinated by the man with the apron who led the Royal Welsh Fusiliers' mascot goat. It seems unlikely that the goat ever went into battle. At the Trooping of the Colour, it is the cavalry wearing aprons and carrying axes who interest me most. But these are not really significant when it comes to winning battles.

c. Professional or non-professional ('tentmakers')

There are parts of the world impossible to enter as a professional missionary: countries such as mainland China, Iraq or Turkey would be obvious examples. There are no countries closed to Christian students, diplomats, business people, technicians and teachers. Some outstanding Christian work has been done in such countries by Christians who work in a secular capacity but make no secret of the reality of their faith in Christ. These are sometimes called 'tentmakers' because they support themselves by their own labours as the apostle Paul did, though their primary reason for being in secular employment is not so much to support themselves as to gain entry for the gospel.

In such countries, non-professional missionaries are a priority. It is different in countries where there are no restrictions on entry. The appointing of Christian PhDs to university posts may achieve little or nothing, unless they possess spiritual gifts that will make them effective soul-winners and trainers. It could be said that such Christian lecturers trying to do two jobs simultaneously need to be more gifted spiritually than a professional Christian worker who is able to concentrate solely on one main task. Selection of

141

such 'tentmakers' therefore needs to be more rigorous, rather than less.

Some years ago Dr Raymond Windsor of BMMF Interserve gave a paper on what he called 'non-missionary professionals'. These would be well-trained medical and paramedical workers who treat patients with professional skill during working hours, but who never learn the language well enough to communicate the gospel, who spend their evenings relaxing in expatriate clubs following a western lifestyle, and whose weekends may be spent enjoying cheap excursions to the Himalayas! Even if such people are recruited by missionary societies, it would be stupid to think of them as true missionaries committed to building Christ's church.

d. Short-term or long-term

Both individuals and churches need to see the priorities here. I am a great believer in short-term missionary work. It is an excellent way of persuading those who go for a short time, and become frustrated by their inability to speak to people in their own language, to go back long-term! There are always cautious people who cannot make up their minds or commit themselves to long-term work until they have first had a look. Once they have seen the scale of the need for evangelism, they will come back determined to give their lives. Short-term work has possibilities in places where English can be understood, but where there is a national language, those who come short-term cannot answer a telephone, read a timetable, understand a service of worship or preach the gospel without an interpreter. There are exceptions of course, and short-term workers may be used to lead the occasional person to Christ (if that person already speaks good English). But for the most part short-term workers are dependent on others to interpret for them. (Often the interpreters could say twice as much in the same time and with more relevance to the culture!) You can treat refugees with kindness and show Christian love without the language, but you cannot preach Christ meaningfully or build up Christians as disciples without the language.

Churches need to consider carefully what they are doing. Are they funding a form of Christian sight-seeing, with earnest spiritual expectations unlikely to be realized, though with real benefits to the individuals enjoying the opportunity? Or are they really making a priority contribution to the building of the church? There is no sense in sending someone to work short-term whom they would not judge to be of sufficient calibre and gift to stay long-term!

A final plea

Churches need to pray and plan together, both for evangelistic outreach in their own neighbourhood and their sending of church members as missionaries to the end of the earth. Many will plan local evangelism with meticulous care, but leave the wider responsibility to a kind of *ad hoc* serendipity that something will work out somehow. This attitude is irresponsible: a church is not an end in itself. Emil Brunner said that a church exists by mission as a fire exists by burning. If that is so, the church that is not involved in mission will soon die out. The church exists to do something on earth, it is *for* something: it must have goals for its mission in the world. We cannot survive as inward-looking, programme-orientated churches.

CHURCH PERFECTING

This is work done by missionaries in local churches once indigenous leaders have been appointed, and the missionary is no longer in charge.

a. Church-pivoted outreach evangelism to found daughter churches.

b. Training of elders in the area.

c. Theological education by extension in the area.

d. Training of Sunday school teachers in the area.

e. Church-pivoted young people's work.

f. Bible reading promotion work (Scripture Union *etc.*).

g. Church-based high-school evangelism.

h. Bible translation and literacy work in the target language.

i. Pastoring a church as an example to local pastors.

j. Church-based literature distribution (shops, bookmobiles).

k. Helping nationals in radio broadcasting *etc.*

l. Para-church work among students, nurses, soldiers *etc.*

THE LEADERSHIP OF THE CHURCH
Who makes the decisions?

It was he who gave some to be apostles, some to be prophets, some to be evangelists, and some to be pastors and teachers, to prepare God's people for works of service, so that the body of Christ may be built up until we all reach unity in the faith and in the knowledge of the Son of God and become mature, attaining to the whole measure of the fulness of Christ. (Eph. 4:11–13)

Be shepherds of God's flock . . . not lording it over those entrusted to you, but being examples to the flock. (1 Pet. 5:2–3)

Jesus called them together and said, 'You know that the rulers of the Gentiles lord it over them, and their high officials exercise authority over them. Not so with you. Instead, whoever wants to become great among you must be your servant . . .' (Mt. 20:25–26)

The greatest danger of the 'successful church' is that it provides a very good show for a huge number of non-involved 'spectators', and that it becomes activity orientated rather than goal orientated.

In an urban Baptist church of 620 members, as many as 53% of those attending were not members of the church. At an independent church, with 480 members, 62% of those who came did not belong.[1]

Let me develop this problem by using an analogy or parable from a rugby football team.

A group of fifteen people decide to form a rugby team. All are very committed to the game, all turn out each week to practise and to play. They play well together and win every match in their first season.

Unfortunately five players leave at the end of the season. Short of three forwards (back row of the scrum) and two wing-threequarters, the team plays gallantly and still succeeds in winning some matches. The club has now been joined by some eager supporters, who, while not actually playing themselves, stand on the touchline and cheer like mad, encouraging the understandably exhausted players.

Five more players leave before the third season starts, so that the club, which now has still more supporters, is left fielding only five players. These play like men demented, with enormous energy in a vain attempt to defend their own line when outnumbered three to one by their opponents. Naturally, they lose every match, and their supporters tend to be somewhat cynical, even critical, offering well-meaning advice from the touchline, mingled with ribald jeers and cat-calls. A great deal of time is spent in the clubhouse reminiscing about the former glories of the team, and eulogizing players who have left.

In the fourth season, four more players leave to join other clubs, as they have become somewhat disheartened. In fact, some of the critical spectators leave with them. But the gallant full-back, who has been a tower of strength in the past, gallops up and down his line in vain attempts to stem the overwhelming attack. He has always been a very good player. It is almost a relief not to have to pass the ball to the others from time to time! He is hopelessly outnumbered and very disheartened by the attitude of the spectators and the club supporters.

In the early days, every member of the club had been a player and participator and had called the team 'we' and 'us'. It was noticeable that the club members now spoke of their team as 'them' or 'it', or even, with only one surviving player, 'him'!

Unfortunately the full-back has a fatal heart attack, and all the remaining fixtures have to be cancelled. Remarkably the club continues its activities, and meets with great faithfulness every Saturday to discuss past matches, and even to talk about playing some more football. They have, in fact, advertised for a new full-back, but for some reason there is a shortage of applicants.

This illustrates what happens in Christian groups when the founding members have all left, and goal-orientation has been lost. Nobody is quite sure why the church meets, but the activity is seen as having some value in itself, and so continues even when the original purpose has been lost!

One of the crucial functions of Christian leadership is to give a sense of direction. The English term 'Those with gifts of administration' (1 Cor. 12:28) is a Greek word (*kybernēseis*), related to another biblical word for 'captain' or 'steersman' (*kybernētēs*, Acts 27:11; Rev. 18:17). The responsibility of Christian leaders is to steer, to set a clear course for a church, and to plan ahead. The members of the congregation (or any other group) need to be briefed about where they are going. Without that kind of leadership, churches degenerate into a round of meetings. The church exists, but nobody is quite sure why!

The true function of ministry

Like many others I would want to draw upon Ephesians 4:11–13 as a basis for ministry. The traditional understanding in the Anglo-Saxon world was based upon the unfortunate placing of commas in the King James version. There is no punctuation of this kind in the original New Testament, and they were added by translators still influenced by a hierarchical view of ministry, as being performed by a clerical class of ministers. Thus it used to seem that apostles, prophets, evangelists and pastors/teachers had a threefold function: to equip the saints; for works of service; and to build up the body.

All three of these functions were carried out by the clerical professionals. The removal of the commas, as expositors like Alan Stibbs pointed out,[2] transformed the whole understanding of this passage. The function of the ministers given by the ascended Christ is that they are slaves to serve his people, 'to equip God's people for works of ministry in order to build up the body of Christ . . .'. Here we no longer have churches where professionals officiate while 'laymen' spectate. There is still an important role for the professionals as equippers, trainers who will see it as their office to get all of God's people engaged in ministry. But they are no longer pulpit prima donnas, they are conductors whose task is to persuade the whole congregation to become participators. They are no longer champion performers, but trainers with the task of training spectators to become players!

Our problem is that traditionally our colleges have expected to train soloists, good preachers and teachers, who lead the congregation. Worse, the mental image of the students themselves and their expectation is that they will become omnicompetent ministers. Very few want to be trained as trainers of others: most are individualists, who like the idea of leading and feel called to teach. Some are not even very keen on the suggestion that they might invite others to share with them in ministry, like the full-back who found it easier not to rely on others!

It makes all the difference when ministers see themselves not as those appointed to do everything on their own, but as activators and enthusers of others: not so much players as coaches and managers; not as the sole preachers in their churches, but as those who have the task of training up a whole company of preachers; not the one person cumbered with a load of visiting, but as a trainer of a whole team of visitors. It requires an entirely different view of the role of the vicar, pastor, minister – and this, not just on the part of the individual leader, but in the attitude of the congregation towards their leader.

Human ordination or God's gifts?

The disagreement between the historic denominations and those who have favoured a gathered-church view has related to the authority of its ministers. The view of Roman Catholics, Lutherans and many Anglicans, for example, has depended upon the belief that episcopal ordination goes back to St Peter and the first apostles. There is thus a godly succession of those upon whom hands have been laid after appropriate theological training. The assumption has then been that such people are adequate preachers, pastors and administrators as a result of their office and training. It is commonly the case, however, that very few are skilled in all three spheres. This theory means that they are thought to possess the skills by virtue of their office or appointment as ministers and their theological study.

By contrast there are those whose ministry is 'charismatic', *i.e.* who have received spiritual gifts, sovereignly given by God, and whose gifts are then recognized by their fellow-Christians. This was the view of the Christian Brethren and the Independents in the past. It is the recognition of their God-given gifts rather than hierarchical status or church appointment that fits them for ministry. They become ministers because God has given to them the skills that fit them for the task.

This contrast can be overdrawn: denominational ministers may be, and indeed ought to be, carefully screened and selected on the basis that they have already shown evidence of spiritual gifts given by God. While theological study has sometimes been academic and irrelevant, there have also been sincere attempts to train men (and a few women) in preaching, pastoral care, and counselling, and even (much less commonly) in church administration and management. It has to be admitted that sometimes they may show little evidence of either spiritual gifts or effective training for teaching, pastoring or administering. Some may be good at one or even two of these activities, yet the assumption is that because of their ordination and training they are legally bound and automatically qualified to do all three. It is a fact of life that those gifted in one area are not necessarily gifted in the others, and sadly a few show little evidence of being gifted in any. The insights of the charismatic movement, based on biblical teaching, suggest that not all these gifts may be found, or should be expected to be found, in the same individuals just because they have been to college, wear some form of clerical dress or are called 'Reverend'.

On the other hand, many of the early leaders of the Christian Brethren movement were ordained ministers with some theological training who reacted against the deadness and institutionalism of the established church. The later anti-intellectualism among Brethren, which assumed that every male who stood to his feet was, by definition, speaking with the help of the Spirit,

and that all of them without exception were charis-
matically gifted as speakers, was possibly among the
main reasons for their decline. It was a painful lesson
that while some had something to say, others just had
to say something, even if it blessed no-one!

It would be true that while some of the leaders in
restorationist groupings have a background in the
Christian Brethren, and are self-taught and sometimes
seem theologically inept (*e.g.* in their failure to recognize that God's Holy Spirit has been active throughout
all church history, and that he did not have to wait for
us to arrive!), others have read widely, and some have
had good theological training.

The truth is that the older denominations have
begun to recognize what the evangelicals among them
have always recognized, that ordination does not make
every person automatically an effective, fruitful minister of God's Word. Charismatic gifts from God have
always been needed (and evangelicals were teaching
that long before the renewal movements began). On
the other hand, experience can be shared and taught,
and so can management skills.

How biblical is ordination?

A good scriptural case can be made out for ordination,
and this goes all the way back to Moses ordaining
Joshua as his successor. The Old Testament accounts
are instructive:

> So the LORD said to Moses, 'Take Joshua son of Nun,
> a man in whom is the Spirit, and lay your hand on
> him. Make him stand before Eleazar the priest and
> the entire assembly and commission him in their
> presence. Give him some of your authority so that the
> whole Israelite community will obey him . . .'
> Moses did as the LORD commanded him. He took

151

Joshua and made him stand before Eleazar the priest and the whole assembly. Then he laid hands on him and commissioned him (Nu. 27:18–23).

Now Joshua son of Nun was filled with the spirit of wisdom because Moses had laid his hands on him (Dt. 34:9).

Moses' 'ordination' of Joshua, a man already possessing the Spirit, was a public commissioning before the people, and this involved giving him authority, and the spirit of wisdom.

Kelly comments about the practice of 'leaning' or 'pressing on' of hands:

This action of laying, or rather pressing, hands on someone (the Hebrew verb is *samakh* . . . is entirely different from the 'placing' (Hebrew verb *sim* or *shith*) of the hands employed for blessings and healings, although the two are commonly confused and rendered by the same Greek verb in both the LXX and the N.T.[3]

In the New Testament there are frequent references to the laying on of hands by church leaders in a congregational setting. Thus the apostles laid hands on Stephen and the others, already known to be full of the Spirit and wisdom (Acts 6:3–6). The leaders of the Antioch church also laid their hands on Barnabas and Saul and sent them out (Acts 13:2). The two most striking references are by Paul writing to Timothy:

Do not neglect your gift *(charismatos)*, which was given you through a prophetic message when the body of elders laid their hands on you (1 Tim. 4:14).

I remind you to fan into flame the gift *(charisma)* of God, which is in you through the laying on of my hands (2 Tim. 1:6).

This was probably the same occasion when both Paul and the elders of the church in Lystra laid hands on Timothy, as he was sent out to work with Paul and Silas (Acts 16:2–3). The word 'ordination' is never used as such, still less the word 'priesthood' in such a context, but it is clear that the early churches commissioned workers by the laying on of hands.

Many of the problems to do with the ordination of women relate much more to the problem of ordination itself, than to the suitability of women. If there is a plural leadership in a congregation, more than half of whom are probably female, it would seem absolute folly not to have some women members involved in consultation and decision. The problem arises when the question really means: 'Do you believe that a woman is qualified to be an omnicompetent, one-woman-band who is the only person in the congregation qualified to preside at the Lord's table, administer baptisms, and pronounce absolutions and blessings?'

It is a conviction that I share with many others, within as well as outside of the older denominational churches, that the church's growth and progress have been seriously impeded because no one individual male ought to be loaded with all of that either. 'One-man-band churches' do not seem to find any support in the New Testament. The whole point of many of the 'body' and 'gifts' passages is that all the members of the body must be actively involved and working properly (Eph. 4:16), in order for the body to grow and upbuild itself. A body with only one member functioning is almost dead. That one organ may be the heart, with the responsibility of pumping blood to make all the other members function, but if it alone is functioning, immediate hospitalization is the only hope!

How biblical is training for ministry?

There seems little doubt that Moses trained Joshua for leadership over many years, that Elijah prepared Elisha to be his successor, that the Lord Jesus taught the Twelve over three years, and that the apostle Paul trained Timothy, in particular, as his letters to him show.

True, it was not a library-centred academic training, but it involved listening to a teacher, studying him in action, being sent out to pass on to others what had been seen, heard and learned, then returning for more teaching. Eventually the teacher was no longer involved but was somewhere else beginning that whole process of teaching and training others once more.

A key passage is 2 Timothy 2, where Timothy is instructed to pass on what he has learned from Paul, to other men (not 'men' in the sense of males, as some translations seem to suggest; we shall look at this later), who are qualified to teach others. The assumption is that not all persons are necessarily so qualified. The point is illustrated by reference to the committed soldier, the athlete who follows the rules (for the Olympic Games there was a minimum requirement of ten months' training!) and the hard-working farmer. All these people who learn from the experience of others: the soldier from his instructors, the athlete from his trainer and the farmer from his father before him.

The possession of charismatic gifts does not make it unnecessary to do personal study or to learn from more experienced people, quite the reverse in fact. Both references to Timothy's *charisma* in the two letters to him remind him that he must not neglect his gift (1 Tim. 4:14) and that he must stir it into flame (2 Tim. 1:6). Mere possession is not enough: it is a gift given by

God certainly, and perhaps associated with the laying on of hands (in both passages), but it must be worked at and exercised. This is very evident in 1 Timothy 4:7–16 where the whole stress of Paul's exhortation is that Timothy is to apply himself diligently to study (notice the verbs 'train yourself', verse 7; 'devote yourself to', verse 13; 'do not neglect', verse 14; 'be diligent in these matters; give yourself wholly to them so that all may see your progress', verse 15; 'persevere', verse 16. A similar emphasis is found in 2 Timothy 2:15: 'Do your best to present yourself to God as one approved, a workman who does not need to be ashamed and who correctly handles the word of truth.'

Scripture clearly teaches that Christian workers need teaching and training themselves first, before they are qualified to teach and train others. There is a need for diligent, persevering study. There is no place for the anti-intellectualist arguments which maintain that a person who has the gifts of the Spirit is automatically programmed and needs no study or training.

Church authority and individual autonomy

During the course of church history, there have been several ways in which the authority of the church has been regarded. The Roman Catholic view gives authority to the priests and supremely to the Pope. The Protestant view was a reaction against this, and stresses that each person must be responsible for his or her own decisions. It derives from Paul's teaching to the Romans: 'Each one should be fully convinced in his own mind. . . . Each of us will give an account of himself to God' (Rom. 14:5, 12).

155

Even though Paul himself had expressed his own views against the keeping of the sabbath (Col. 2:16) and concern over unclean food (1 Cor. 10:25), he could not and would not compel others to accept his own position. He saw that each believer must be fully convinced in his or her own mind, and that each of us is answerable to the Lord alone, and not to humans.

This 'right of private judgment' was one of the great issues of the Reformation. To go back to authoritative leaders, whose teaching must be accepted, is a return to popery and a denial of our Protestant heritage. The submission that the New Testament teaches is never mere acceptance of orders from above, right or wrong, but the free, intelligent recognition of the authentic autonomy of other believers led by the Spirit. It is not treating church members as though they are 'sheep' with no minds of their own.

It is not unusual for demands for absolute submission to be bolstered with words of 'prophecy'. But Scripture commands that all such should be 'weighed' 'judged' or 'tested', and when sincere believers are full of doubts, this is not unbelief or wilfulness, but an important part of the 'weighing' process. There is a considerable spectrum of options available: it is not a simple choice between anarchy and popery! And I am using the word 'popery' just as much of extreme Protestant authoritarianism, as of any Catholic or episcopal form.

SPECTRUM OF CHURCH AUTHORITY AND INDIVIDUAL AUTONOMY

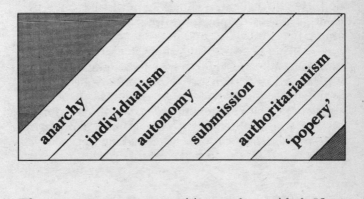

anarchy · individualism · autonomy · submission · authoritarianism · 'popery'

There are two extreme positions to be avoided. If we over-emphasize the authority of the church, then the individual is in danger of becoming like a programmed computer with no ideas of his own, no doctrinal understanding or spiritual depth, meekly submitting to the current view of his subcultural ghetto-mates. 'It is the teaching of my church', he cries, escaping responsibility for his beliefs or actions.

The opposite extreme is the individual who is answerable to no-one. 'The Lord has told me . . .' he insists.

I remember a student who had failed a degree course disastrously, and needed to be steered to a much less demanding course. His gifts were not academic but were of a practical and pastoral nature. However, he insisted that 'the Lord has told me that I should spend another year, repeating the whole course'. It was very difficult to persuade him that his guidance was based on a false view of what success as a Christian means.

Or there is the spiritual blackmail of the courting

male who says, 'The Lord tells me that I must marry you!' so that the girl, who is not attracted to him in the least, is made to seem or feel unspiritual if she turns him down. We can see that the traditional Protestant view could produce a chaotic situation, in which each individual becomes a 'pope' doing what is right in his own eyes.

How do we resolve this tension? Not by turning every church pastor and elder into a local mini-pope. The Christian disciple then loses his autonomy: he becomes no longer a disciple of Jesus, owing allegiance and obedience to him alone, but a disciple of his pastor. It places on the minister the intolerable burden of 'playing God' in the lives of others, and making decisions for people that they should make for themselves.

Discipline and shepherding

The authoritarian 'shepherding' teaching found in some of the house churches has been heavily criticized. But we need to understand that it springs from a desire to make discipleship a matter of obedience, and not merely obeying when we feel like it. The Methodist class meeting in the past brought group pressure upon the individual to shun temptation and to seek holiness, aided by the approval or disapproval of the group (like a kind of spiritual Weightwatchers!). The Catholic practice of having a spiritual director has recently found some revived interest among Protestants.[4]

But discipleship and obedience are not options. To be answerable to an older Christian, and for each of us to receive help, encouragement and rebuke in order to make progress in spiritual growth, are not wrong, provided they are seen as a form of voluntary subjection. This background to 'covering' or 'shepherding' should help us to appreciate the worthy and spiritual motivation which lies behind it.[5]

In these house churches, a father shepherds his own family, and in turn is helped by some senior Christian, who is shepherded by his pastor, who in turn is also ministered to by an itinerant 'apostle'. This concept can be helpful, provided it is recognized that there can be no absolute authority over the life of another, who is answerable only to his own master. Some attempts to derive this structure from Old Testament kingship or from delegation of authority by Moses do seem a little far-fetched. Neither does there seem to be any New Testament warrant for the structure, though there would seem to be plenty for admonition, rebuke and discipline. But when the Protestant minister becomes more authoritative than any Catholic priest, a little local pope, there is a failure to recognize that church leaders are fallible human beings capable of making silly, stupid decisions as well as wise ones.

> Undenominational
> But still the church of God
> He stood in his conventicle
> And ruled it with a rod.
>
> (John Betjeman)

The Lord Jesus specifically forbids his disciples to follow secular, authoritarian leadership styles familiar from the world around them, as we now see.

New Testament leadership style

The Lord Jesus contrasted leadership among his people both with Gentile secular leadership: 'The rulers of the Gentiles lord it over them, and their high officials exercise authority over them. *Not so with you*' (Mt. 20:25–26). He also drew a contrast with Jewish religious leadership style: 'But you are *not* to be called "Rabbi", for you have only one Master and you are all brothers'

159

(Mt. 23:8–11). Peter actually takes one of these unpleasant words to describe Gentile leadership, reminiscing on the words of the Lord Jesus, when he writes to elders: 'Not lording it over those entrusted to you, but being examples to the flock' (1 Pet. 5:3). Thus the New Testament teaches that the Christian style of leadership is different both from secular and religious authority models. In both contexts there is a contrast with the humble service of a servant or even a slave, who leads not by exercising authority, but by setting an example.

Romans 14 shows that even though he possessed apostolic authority, Paul did not use his authority to insist that people should accept his views on the keeping of days, eating kosher food, drinking and so on. He makes the point that each of us must make up his or her own mind, and each of us will one day have to give an account to God of the decisions we have made: we cannot plead that we accepted the teaching of our church, or our leaders. We are responsible for our own decisions.

Much more thought needs to be given to the development of a truly Christian style of leadership, modelled on the New Testament rather than on our cultural Gentile or religious models!

Congregational authority

But there is authority in the congregation, not in any one individual, however spiritual or theologically well-educated. It is worth commenting that those inclined to be over-authoritative are sometimes making up for not having much theological education, and, feeling threatened, tend to overcompensate! The true authority is found in the group.

Matthew 18:15–20 has traditionally been understood to be about two or three praying together, but this has been questioned recently,[6] and a convincing case has been made that the passage is about Christ's presence in settling matters of dispute and discipline. The individual ought to listen to the two or three (though as a mini-faction within the subculture, they too could be wrong), but he must listen to the church (*i.e.* the assembled saints). Here is the moderate, safe, middle way between dictatorship by one individual and whimsy on the part of the many. We need to submit to the advice and experience of others, though the final decision must still be ours. 'Obey your leaders' (Heb. 13:17) may certainly be quoted, but there is a plurality of leadership and this gives no authority to local popes. There are always limits to authority exercised by individuals in Scripture, whether government, husbands or leaders within the churches. The apostles did not hesitate when they had sound biblical reasons to disagree with the leaders of Israel. Paul did not hesitate to oppose the apostle Peter to the face when Peter was clearly in the wrong in Antioch (Gal. 2:11; Paul thus opposed James of Jerusalem too, if less directly). There are limits to authority. It is never, 'Obey your leaders right or wrong, however stupid'. That is why in Romans 14:4 Paul insists that each of us is finally answerable to God alone.

The ministry of women

Recently I wrote a book called *Serving Grace: Gifts Without Inverted Commas*,[7] which contains a chapter that seeks to answer the question whether God gives women all the charismatic gifts given to men, or only some of them. I can comment briefly here upon only three gifts, which can be enumerated as follows:

> God has appointed first of all apostles, second prophets, third teachers (1 Cor. 12:28).

161

It is clear that the Twelve were all men. But what about that lesser group also known as apostles, that included Barnabas, Silas and Timothy, Epaphroditus, Andronicus and Junia?

The last named was, it seems, regarded as a female apostle by all the early church fathers. A most interesting recent article discusses Junia or Junias in some detail.[8] Suffice it to say that until the ninth or tenth century Junias was written in Greek without any accent, and was taken as being feminine. From that time on it was printed with an acute accent, indicating that it was a first declension noun and thus still feminine. As recently as 1958, it appeared for the very first time with an acute accent as a shortened form of a masculine name, in the second edition of the Bible Society text. One wonders who authorized that alteration in the text!

Another recent careful discussion was that of C. E. B. Cranfield in his masterly two-volume commentary on the Greek text of Romans. He first points out gently that the suggestion of earlier commentators, Sanday and Headlam, that Junias was 'less usual as a man's name' is misleading, for it is found nowhere else as a man's name, so that we cannot know that it is a man's name in Romans 16:7 unless we have already decided that it is! So he sums up by saying: 'It is surely right to assume that the person referred to was a woman'.[9]

There are other women that Paul commands as members of the same team (Phil. 4:3 'contended at my side') and as his colleagues (Phil. 4:3; Rom. 16:3, 'fellow-workers'). There are also the four women – Mary, Tryphena, Tryphosa and Persis who are all said to 'labour', a word Paul uses elsewhere for the work of leaders and his own apostolic work. However this is the only woman, whose name we know, who is called an apostle.

When we look at the next word, 'prophets', the situation is quite different. There are several unequivocal

162

general comments about women prophesying – as in the Pentecost quotation of Joel 2:28, 'Your sons and daughters will prophesy' (Acts 2:17), while Paul tells the Corinthian church that 'every woman who prays or prophesies with her head uncovered dishonours her head'. This assumes that women do prophesy, which also seems implied by the later statement, 'for you can all prophesy in turn' (1 Cor. 11:5; 14:31). We know of Philip's four prophesying daughters in Caesarea, though we do not know their names (Acts 21:9). We are told that the aged Anna was a prophetess (Lk. 2:36), while in the previous chapter both Elizabeth and Mary seem to have prophesied in the power of the Spirit (Lk. 1:41f.; 46ff.).

There seems no doubt, then, that in the New Testament as in the Old (Miriam, Deborah and Huldah), there were women who exercised this gift.

The third gift mentioned is teaching, and our immediate response is that Paul quite explicitly forbids women to teach (1 Tim. 2:12). But it is possible that we have misunderstood and mistranslated him. The words interpreted there as 'women . . . man' can equally well be read (as they are in many other places) 'wife . . . husband'. That the apostle would not allow a wife to teach or domineer over her husband seems an equally permissible way of reading the text, especially in view of the commendation of women workers in Romans 16 and 2 Timothy 2:2.

In the latter text, the apostle seems deliberately to avoid speaking of 'faithful *males* who will be able to teach others also'. If the apostle really intended that teaching should be confined to males, he could have clarified the issue for ever by using the word *androi* here. He does not do so, but uses instead the word *anthrōpoi*, meaning 'persons' or 'humans'. Elsewhere older women are commended to teach the younger women (Tit. 2:4); Timothy was taught by his mother and grandmother (2 Tim. 3:15). It appears that Priscilla instructed Apollos in Acts 18:26 where Priscilla's name again appears first before that of Aquila, her husband.

Some also think it possible that the phrase 'I do not permit a woman/wife . . .' in 1 Timothy 2:12 may refer to some specific woman or wife, who was causing trouble in Ephesus, rather than 'a woman' in a generic sense. But what is forbidden is not female teaching in general (allowed in 2 Tim. 2:2) but the heretical teaching of certain Jewish myths. These held that Eve, as the 'mother of all living' (Gn. 3:20), must have been created *before* Adam and that it was Adam, not Eve, who was deceived.[10] It is therefore a misunderstanding to see this as a general ban on the ministry of women. It is, rather, an *ad hoc* ruling outlawing heretical gnostic teaching in Ephesus, where mother-goddess cults were rampant. Reading 1 Timothy 2:12 as a general ban on the ministry of women raises problems because it does not harmonize with passages like Romans 16 where Paul writes commending the ministry of women. Not only must the apostle be consistent, but, much more important, Scripture must be consistent with itself.

There is not space to take this discussion further here, but what we have looked at so far suggests that the meaning of 1 Timothy 2 is far from being as cut and dried as some men (and women) have assumed. The problem is not whether women should be set aside for some kind of Christian ministry (Rom. 16 and Phil. 4 make it clear that the early church certainly did do that), but with the concept of ordination itself, whether of men or women. Some wrongly assume that the 'celebrating priest' at the communion has to be male. A woman, they believe, cannot say the 'magic words' because the priest represents Christ, and therefore must be male. There does not seem to be any convincing biblical argument against women being set apart by the church for full-time ministry.

All those who have had the privilege of working with

female colleagues in overseas mission, as I have, must bear testimony not only to their commitment, but to their exercise of spiritual gifts of teaching. Hudson Taylor, commenting on his women colleagues, said they were 'the most powerful agency at our disposal'.

And I would want to add that any church that does not set aside women for some kind of ministry is both denying the priesthood of all believers and questioning the wisdom of God in giving grace and gifts of grace to women.

Conclusion

A great variety of words are used as descriptive of leadership in the various churches in the New Testament. They are called 'elders' in Acts and the Pastorals; 'leaders' in Acts and Hebrews; 'apostles' and 'administrators' (a word close to that used elsewhere for a steersman) in the lists of spiritual gifts in Corinthians; and Romans and Thessalonians speak of 'those who lead' or 'are over you' (*prohistamenoi*). This suggests that there was greater flexibility in names and structures than we sometimes imagine when we try to construct a single system that we would like to describe as *the* New Testament doctrine of ministry. It seems that leaders were called different names in different churches (just as secular leaders had a variety of different titles). There is no New Testament Leviticus prescribing one form of organization, even if earnest brethren have tried to remedy this 'deficiency' in Scripture ever since! If the sovereign Spirit did not see fit to give us such detailed instructions for church order and organization, then we had far better go on doing without. Leadership, decency and order we must have, but we do not have to compel our brothers and sisters in other congregations to do things exactly as we do, as though ours was the only correct way.

165

chapter nine

THE PARA-CHURCH MOVEMENTS AND THE CHURCH
When is a church not a church?

Some of them, however, men from Cyprus and Cyrene, went to Antioch and began to speak to Greeks also, telling them the good news about the Lord Jesus. (Acts 11:20)

Some time later Paul said to Barnabas, 'Let us go back and visit the brothers in all the towns where we preached the word of the Lord and see how they are doing.' Barnabas wanted to take John, also called Mark, with them, but Paul did not think it wise to take him, because he had deserted them in Pamphylia and had not continued with them in the work.

They had such a sharp disagreement that they parted company. Barnabas took Mark and sailed for Cyprus, but Paul chose Silas and left, commended by the brothers to the grace of the Lord. He went through Syria and Cilicia, strengthening the churches.

He came to Derbe and then to Lystra, where a disciple named Timothy lived, whose mother was a Jewess and a believer, but whose father was a Greek. The brothers at Lystra and Iconium spoke well of him. Paul wanted to take him along on the journey, so he circumcised him because of the Jews who lived in that area, for they all knew that his father was a Greek. As they travelled from town to town, they delivered the decisions reached by the apostles and elders in Jerusalem for the people to obey. So the churches were strengthened in the faith and grew daily in numbers. (Acts 15:36 – 16:5)

'Ataxia' is defined in the Oxford Dictionary as 'inability to control the voluntary movements'. Certainly times of spiritual revival and ferment have always resulted in a proliferation of new 'voluntary' movements – missions and societies. The *UK Christian Handbook 1987–88* analyses all the Christian organizations listed and says that the proportion of new organizations started since 1960 has risen from 45% in 1982 to 55% in 1986, and no less than 60% of all these organizations are inter-denominational.[1]

From an institutional viewpoint this is unsanctified individualism and this chaotic proliferation of new organizations seems like cancerous growths upon the body of Christ. Seen from another viewpoint, however, this is where the life of the church has always been, the 'free enterprise' or even the 'privatization' of aspects of the church's activity. Those who are involved in the denominational bureaucracies easily develop a kind of 'civil service' mentality and the wheels of ecclesiastical organization do seem to move very slowly indeed. Eager, impatient, free spirits then endeavour to speed things up by private initiatives in starting fresh structures.

The situation becomes more complex when there is not just one large 'state church' as in Norway or Sweden, but several large denominational structures – Anglican, Presbyterian, Methodist and URC. Life is too short to wait for them to act together, so there seems to be a great deal of sense in some interdenominational activity which can operate independently of denominational bureaucracy.

What is the relationship between voluntary movements (college and office Christian Unions, missionary societies, *etc.*) and the churches?

There is no doubt that these 'para-church' organizations, as they are often called, have been a source of blessing and life to the churches. But, being the result of the independent exercise of a group of concerned

168

Christians, they are quite deliberately outside normal church structures, and often call themselves specifically 'interdenominational'. Actually 'supra-denominational' or 'non-denominational' is usually a much more accurate term, though bodies like the British Council of Churches could be called 'co-denominational'.

Ralph Winter, in a famous article, described churches and para-church organizations, respectively as 'modalities and sodalities'. While you might think that introducing two new and unfamiliar long words doesn't help very much, in fact it does.[2]

A church is a *modality* – it has no limitations of age or sex, you do not retire from it at a certain age, you belong to only one church at a time, and it contains whole families.

A para-church group is a *sodality* – defined as 'a religious guild or brotherhood established for purposes of devotion or mutual help or action'.[3] They are voluntary and usually rather loose associations, which exist for a precise and limited purpose. They may be limited just to men, or to women, to students, or to business people. It may be a Bible college, a missionary society to evangelize China, to translate the Bible, to evangelize students, or to mobilize Christian women. People may belong to more than one such group. Para-church sodalities have always been a better way of getting things done. Even a monolithic church with a heirarchical structure like the Roman Catholic Church found that orders like the Franciscans or the Jesuits were able to get action much more quickly than the church as a whole.

There was a great spate of new missionary societies started in Britain at the end of the eighteenth century:

Baptist Missionary Society (1792)
London Missionary Society (1795)
Church Missionary Society (1799)
British and Foreign Bible Society (1804)

169

All of these, except the Bible Society, were denominational in character. But it was not the denominational church bodies as such which helped get these organizations started, rather it was small groups of committed individuals. In due course the organizations were accepted as part of the establishment. For example, the Church Missionary Society was formed by sixteen Anglican clergymen and nine laymen who met on 12 April 1799 at the Castle and Falcon Inn in Aldersgate Street. It was 'a society amongst the members of the established church for sending missionaries among the heathen'. It was Charles Simeon's instigation and the persistent persuasion of William Wilberforce, John Venn, Charles Grant and others that gave rise to 'The Society for Missions to Africa and the East', as it was called at first.[4] This society sprang from the Eclectic Society, founded by John Newton of St Mary Woolnoth in 1783. Originally it was limited to thirteen evangelical clergy or laity working in London, and later came the addition of thirteen country members from 1798 of whom Charles Simeon was one.[5]

It would be fair to say that evangelicalism in the Church of England owes its survival to a whole series of such para-church societies, while the energies of earnest committed Christians found an outlet of the kind often denied them in the institutionalized churches. The energies of Christian women for so long denied opportunity of service within official church structures, also found expression in para-church work.

Are para-church groups scriptural?

Some para-church groups have demanded such total

commitment from members that they have usurped the place of church involvement, holding Sunday meetings, and in some cases, such as the Salvation Army, becoming a denomination demanding a total lifestyle commitment from its members.

There have always been those who questioned the status and validity of all para-church organizations. The Roman Catholic Church struggled with the powerful orders within its own ranks. More exclusive Christian Brethren, as well as some Reformed and Restorationist churches, have occasionally urged their members to withdraw from school and university Christian Unions, Scripture Union, Youth for Christ and so on. One Restoration church group signed up a whole Christian Union into its own membership – it was then no longer a union of Christians from different churches uniting for a limited purpose of evangelism and training, but a denominational student group. Other denominational groups have formed their own student groups, fearing that they will be influenced by Christians from other traditions.

Those of us familiar with interdenominational Christian activity would be astonished to discover the suspicion and hostility with which such groups are regarded in countries where denominational walls are high. In Japan, for example, para-church groups are careful never to arrange meetings which conflict with Sunday services (which means conferences have to be mid-week rather than at weekends). And in Korea, interdenominational movements are regarded with suspicion and denominations have founded competing organizations of their own.

This raises the important issue of whether, biblically, sodalities have any right to exist. For example, what biblical warrant is there for missionary societies? Do organizations independent of the churches have any right to exist? Let us look at what the Bible has to say about sodalities.

1. While such groups cannot be regarded as 'local churches' they are still part of the universal church. The New Testament recognizes the existence of groups of two and three which are not meetings of the local church (Mt. 18:15–20) and Christians are called not 'to give up meeting together' but to exhort one another 'daily' (Heb. 10:25; 3:13). These passages suggest that Christian small-group activity was a feature of first-century church life also. It seems unlikely that the whole congregation could meet as a local church in plenary session every day. Factory, office and college CUs would seem to fall within this scriptural category.

2. Even in the Old Testament there is evidence of sodalities that functioned outside of the priesthood and levitical structures. One obvious example is the 'company of the prophets' recorded at the time of Elijah and Elisha (2 Ki. 2:3, 5, 7, 15; 4:1, 38; 5:22; 6:1): a sodality limited to prophets, presumably men, though we know some of them were married. Another example is the separation of those who were especially committed, those 'who feared the Lord' and spoke often with one another (Mal. 3:16), particularly in days of apostasy and spiritual declension. The very existence of groups like the *ḥasidim* (lit. 'godly people'), passionately devoted to the Torah and refusing to compromise with the Hellenization of Israel,[6] is a demonstration of this. They developed into the Pharisees, perhaps meaning 'separatists', a party of the most dedicated and committed.

3. In the New Testament, the outstanding example of sodalities would be 'certain men of Cyprus and Cyrene' who first evangelized Antioch and who began preaching to Gentiles with results richly blessed by God. It was an independent lay movement by Hellenistic Jewish Christians, and not, in the first instance, initiated or approved by the leaders and apostles in Jerusalem, who seem to have sent Barnabas to check up on what they were doing up there (Acts 11:19–24). Fortunately, as the writer of Acts makes clear, they already had a

precedent set by the apostle Peter in baptizing Cornelius under the clear guidance of the Spirit, but initially without the approval of the Jerusalem church.

This kind of situation was to be repeated again and again in subsequent church history of Spirit-motivated initiatives taken first by individuals and small groups, used and blessed by God, and then finding favour with the churches. It has been especially true at times when the churches were apostate and spiritually in decline. Reforming movements have all begun as sodalities: Wyclif and the Lollards, the Reformers, the Wesleys, the Christian Brethren and so on, though many of these became modalities.

The goal of para-church movements

It needs to be strongly emphasized, however, that the criterion for the success of an interdenominational group is the extent to which it contributes towards the building up of the church. Take a university Christian Union, for example. The test of its effectiveness is not the number of students who belong to it, or even the proportion of its membership who have been converted through its ministry (though that is very important). The test is long term, and is in the extent to which its former members are now integrated into and playing a part in the leadership of the local church. There is no justification for such movements merely in themselves: they must all be judged by the criterion of the benefits which they bring to the churches.

There is always the temptation for such movements to think that they exist for their own glory and seek to build up their own organization. Individualists ambitious for empire-building may seek to start their own interdenominational movements, or to start new missions, not because of a lack in that field already, but because of wrong ambitions to make a mark and achieve eminence. The same 'tycoon complex' that makes some people successful builders of business empires can result in new Christian organizations. In Korea every pastor seems to want to put up a bigger building, start his own Bible college, establish his own missionary society. Wanting to build our own structures with ourselves on top is a weak doctrine of the church: beware the 'Dallas syndrome'!

I once met an American brother who belonged to a mission of which he and his wife were the only members. The mission was somewhat grandiloquently called World Harvesters Inc., and specialized in putting gospel advertisements into newspapers. This man told me he thought the world needed more Hudson Taylors. To which I replied, somewhat mischievously, that I thought we had had rather too many people with ambitions to start new societies!

Benefits to the church brought by para-church activity

a. Concentration of forces in places of work

No local church is usually large enough to produce a viable Christian group in a factory, office or college: a group uniting people from several congregations will be more effective.

b. Doors closed to local churches are open to interdenominational groups

A denominational church as such may have neither the right nor the personnel to function on a polytechnic or university campus, for example. However well-intentioned, church members are not indigenous to the campus in the way that students are. An inter-denominational fellowship of those who have a right to be on the campus because they study there may be able to cut far more ice than a single local church can, simply by virtue of its non-partisan stance and the fact of belonging to the campus. Other places like factories, hospitals and prisons may be more welcoming to a group which represents more than one denomination.

c. Experience of leadership for younger people

Very properly those who are 'elders' in a local church are usually those who are older in years. This can often be frustrating for gifted younger people who have to wait many years before being appointed to church leadership. School and college Christian Unions give leadership experience and a sense of responsibility to young people which will equip them for service later in the local church. My own first experience of spiritual leadership was in a school Christian Union of around seventy members, when I was seventeen. At university, committee membership and then leadership of a CU, five hundred members of which I knew by name, was invaluable training. In our early twenties we were aware of the great responsibility for evangelizing the university. Consequently we also felt responsible for training the CU members up to be useful, fruitful soul-winners in the missionfield of the student world, and to be useful church members for the rest of our lives.

d. It enables a focus on a particular field of concern

A single local congregation may not have a sufficient number of members interested in mission work in the Andes or Zambesi, or in the defence of the unborn child, or in helping unwed mothers. Such work is much more sensibly undertaken by a para-church movement which enables many different churches to pool their resources, both financially and in terms of interested personnel.

e. It enables members of different churches to relate and co-operate

While it is not easy to provide opportunities for whole local congregations to relate to each other, there is a problem in knowing how members of one local church may relate to those in other churches. One of the beneficial effects of para-church activity in the war years was that people who had known only their own congregation were forced to have fellowship with those from other churches, and could then benefit from the experience and background of others.

f. It enables members to enjoy a convention or celebration ministry

A local church may be relatively small, and with only a few gifted speakers, teachers or musicians. The Keswick Convention provides a place where there can be a spiritual challenge to commitment year by year, with a variety of speakers from different traditions. Spring Harvest again provides an opportunity both to hear a wider variety of ministry than any one local church normally enjoys, and also at the same time the opportunity to participate in celebration with many other believers. It provides for the Christian a spiritual equivalent of the football match, the athletic meeting, or the Promenade Concerts, when large numbers may gather together and rejoice in a human social way, but before God. These may be relatively small occasions compared with those described in the book of Revelation, but they give a small foretaste of them.

g. It provides expertise not possessed by any one local church

When groups are formed to deal with social or other issues, they can draw informed people from a variety of churches which no one local church is able to call upon. Christian Impact is one illustration.

176

h. It provides opportunities for evangelism

Para-church activity provides a neutral opportunity for proclaiming the gospel among special groups of people who may be difficult to reach through church services. A sitting-room or lecture room provides a non-threatening setting for the gospel to be preached, avoiding the anxiety that church services can cause for some people who are uncertain of what is expected of them and are embarrassed at being made to sing the words of hymns they don't know and do not yet accept.

i. It provides services on a scale impossible to the local church

The provision of Bibles by the Bible Society or the publishing of a whole range of books at economic prices are two very obvious examples of the way para-church groups can bring benefit to the church. The progress of a local church may actually be hindered if it is expected to be responsible for expensive projects on too large a scale for them to handle. Moved by the giving of the early church (Acts 4:34–37), generous Chinese Christians embarrassed the 'Little Flock' church by giving businesses, printing works and so on to the church. It is never a kindness for a missionary society to present Christian hospitals to an indigenous church, because it does not have the financial resources to manage such things. Interdenominational para-church groups can provide the resources that are needed for larger projects.

j. It provides channels through which local churches are connected

Strictly speaking, centralized denominational structures are also para-church organizations. They perform useful functions, keeping congregations in touch with each other and widening their interests far beyond immediate parochial concerns. At the same time, because they are part of the establishment, they carry more authority than the usual run of para-church sodalities. Their essential para-church character is much clearer in Christian groups which believe in the autonomy of the local congregation – so that the structures of the Baptist Union, the older Congregational Union or the 'Echoes of Service' office (which provides a loose liaison structure for the sending out of Brethren missionaries) are much more clearly sodalities.

Those churches arranged upon presbyterian or episcopalian organizational structures would see themselves as being 'church' rather than 'para-church'. The episcopalian pattern reflects the ecclesiastical version of the feudal system (the concept of bishops as 'lords' in flagrant contradiction of Mt. 20:25 reflects this), and the presbyterian pattern reflects the oligarchic form of government found in the old city states of Switzerland. One could also say that the Independent Bible Church in North America reflects the social pattern of rugged American individualism and independence. How then do they differ from all other para-church sodalities? Because their authority is recognized by the local churches within that specific form of church order in a way that the more usual independent para-church group is not.

Depending on our view of the relationships between the local church and other churches, within the universal church, we may or may not recognize the validity of their authority. They are none the less human structures, as we argued in chapter 3, and therefore just as fallible as other church and para-church structures, in spite of their age and respectability.

When is a church not a church?

Those meeting in student Christian Unions or in Bible college chapels sometimes find themselves discussing whether or not they are a 'church'. Some years ago under the influence of some strong-minded clinical medical students, the Christian Union at one of the London teaching hospitals declared itself to be 'a church', and started holding Sunday services including communion services. Attached to a hospital, it included nurses and physiotherapists as well as medical students, who by virtue of the length of their courses, were more mature than the general run of university student. In view of all the time-pressure upon those working and studying in hospitals, at first sight this might have seemed to be a helpful development. But it raised several questions.

What if one is already a member of another local church? Does this mean that one has to withdraw from it, or from the hospital 'church'? And if one has denominational convictions – Anglican, Methodist or Baptist – how are these to be included within this new un-denominational church structure? Will it baptize adult believers or babies, or both? Similar problems were raised recently when all the members of a college CU joined a Reformed church and, in another instance, when the students all became members of a house-church. What if one already belongs to some other church with differing convictions on baptism or church-order? The Christian Union is clearly a para-church group involving people of very different denominational persuasions who join together for a limited purpose – evangelizing nurses, soldiers or students. However, if it then joins a church *en masse*, it then ceases to be a Christian *Union* any longer.

Taking the matter further, we confront the much more fundamental issue of what makes a church properly a church by biblical standards, rather than being only a para-church structure?

THE MARKS OF A LOCAL CHURCH

'the total community . . . in local circumscription'[7]

a.	Location	1 Cor. 1:2; 1 Thes.1:1
b.	Organization/structure	Tit. 1:5; Acts 14:23
c.	Authority	Acts 13:1–3; 14:23
d.	Discipline	Acts 20:28; 1 Thes. 5:12–13; Heb. 13:17
e.	Initiation	1 Cor. 1:13–17; 1 Cor. 12:13; 1 Cor. 14–16
f.	Communion	Acts 2:42; 1 Cor. 11:18ff.
g.	Teaching	Col. 1:28; 1 Tim. 4:13
h.	Spiritual gifts	1 Cor. 12:7, 27; 14:12, 26
i.	Families	Eph. 5:21–22; 1 Tim. 3:4; Tit. 1:6
j.	Universal membership	Gal. 3:28; Rom. 14:1; Jas. 2:1–4
k.	Missionary sending	Acts 13:2; 16:2
l.	Giving for others	Acts 11:29–30; 24:17; 1 Cor. 16:1–3

a. Location

A *local* church can be described, for example, as 'the church of God which is in Corinth' (1 Cor. 1:2) or as 'the church of the Thessalonians' (1 Thes. 1:1). Thus the group of those believers travelling with Paul on the ship, carrying the collection for the Jerusalem saints, are an *ad hoc* gathering of believers from several different local churches. They are not called 'the church on the ship' even though all are members of the universal church.

Our fragmented and divided church pattern that causes some people to travel many miles to attend a local church seems far less than ideal. There is so much to be said for being within walking distance of the meeting-place of our local church, so that we meet one another each day as we go out shopping in a natural community, rather than these eclectic congregations travelling miles to get to church.

b. Organization/structure

It is interesting in Acts 14:23 that what were referred to earlier as groups of 'disciples' are not actually called 'churches' until some sort of leadership structure has been appointed. Paul, instructing Titus, seems to feel that there is unfinished business until leadership has been established: 'The reason that I left you in Crete was that you might straighten out what was left unfinished and appoint elders in every town as I directed you' (Tit. 1:5). There must be some decency and order. In writing to the Colossians Paul actually uses the military metaphor, and this is seen in Lightfoot's translation of it as 'beholding your orderly array and close phalanx (solid front)'.[8] A drill sergeant would go berserk at the sloppy, slovenly disorder of some loose aggregations of Christians! There must be a clear structure with a recognized leadership. Usually in para-church groups all that is needed is a committee to organize a programme of events. A church, however, ought to have much clearer goals, and needs a clear structure if it is to be goal-orientated and not programme orientated.

c. Authority

The chaos of a church where everyone does what is right in his own eyes is like that of a centipede whose hundred legs each try to walk in a different direction at once. There must be a recognized leadership which is accepted. The leadership of the apostles is clear in Acts 6:2–3 as they request the membership as a whole to select the Seven, on whom they then lay their hands. In Antioch, the five prophets and teachers (Acts 13:1–3) clearly had recognized authority in setting aside two of their number and sending them off as missionary apostles.

181

They in turn had authority to appoint elders in each of the churches which they had founded (Acts 14:23). When someone is sick, it is not left to any independent set of cowboys to lay hands on him or her at their own volition, which can lead to all manner of problems if the individual is not healed: but the individual must *ask* for the elders to come and lay hands on him or her (Jas. 5:14).

d. Discipline

There has to be vigilance in watching over the flock in view of the dangers to which it is exposed (Acts 20:28). Christians are commanded to respect those over them, who admonish them (1 Thes. 5:12–13). Indeed they are commanded to obey them as those who must give account (Heb. 13:17). Such discipline may involve temporary excommunication of the unrepentant Christian by the church (1 Cor. 5:1–5), public rebuke (1 Tim. 5:19–20), or putting a divisive individual under a ban (Tit. 3:9–11). Some churches have failed for so long to grapple with discipline that they have very little experience or procedure for dealing with it. On the other hand, others are over-ready to discipline those disliked by a threatened, inadequate leadership, because they fail to agree with them on every point.

e. Initiation

Para-church groups have no authority to baptize, and it is in the administration of baptism, to infants where a covenant theology is thought to be biblical, and to believing adults on profession of faith, that we find a significant mark of the church.

It is interesting that though he was an apostle, Paul seems to have expected baptisms to be carried out by local church leaders once he had himself baptized the first two or three households (1 Cor. 1:13–17). And baptism was then expected to be the universal experience of members of the congregation (1 Cor. 12:13). Certainly in the New Testament, there seems to be no

182

such thing as an unbaptized Christian, and baptism seems to have followed immediately on profession of repentance and faith: the longest delay being three days for the apostle Paul (Acts 9:18; 22:16).

f. Communion

The breaking of bread seems to have been a regular feature in the Jerusalem church (Acts 2:42) and a central feature of gatherings of other early churches (1 Cor. 11:18ff.). Here again is a classic mark of the local church, although para-church groups often do conduct communion services at conferences and on significant occasions as a mark of their fellowship together. Anglo-Catholic churches and Brethren assemblies see the communion service as central to their congregational life, and Emil Brunner in his book, *The Misunderstanding of the Church*, argued strongly for its centrality.[9] The breaking of bread is certainly an outstanding mark of the church.

g. Teaching

The teaching gift is frequently referred to as being characteristic of the ministry of elders (1 Tim. 5:17), and of apostolic delegates like Timothy (1 Tim. 4:13), as well as of the apostles themselves (Col. 1:28; Acts 20:20). It is stressed as one of the four marks of Jerusalem church practice (Acts 2:42). As we have seen already in chapter 7, the church comes together for teaching and upbuilding (rather than worship, as such).

> We may go further and say that these meetings of worship had precisely the dominating purpose of building up the Body of Christ. The assemblies were edifying, not in our colourless sense of the word, but in the strict and literal sense of building up.[10]

The recent stress upon prophecy must not be allowed to supersede either the expository teaching of scriptures that have been publicly read or the systematic teaching which is also needed (1 Tim. 4:13). It is plain from the context that diligent preparation and persevering study are a necessary environment for the teaching gift, as it was in exilic days for Ezra the scribe (Ezr. 7:10–11). While teaching may be important in some para-church groups, it is essential in the local church.

h. Spiritual gifts

Peter states the centrality of these in his letter to the refugee Christians in Asia Minor (1 Pet. 4:10–11), stated simply as both verbal and non-verbal in character. The illustration of the body, in which the many members and organs are all necessary and active for the benefit and upbuilding of the whole, is used in Ephesians, Romans and in greatest detail in 1 Corinthians. Brunner stresses that every meeting was 'of such a character that co-operative action in fellowship might be regarded as its decisive feature. It is especially emphasised that *all* were active in it'.[11] No Christian activity can operate without the work of the Holy Spirit pouring his grace into Christians, so that their ministry is an outflow in grace-gifts. Such gifts are exercised in the para-church scene, but they are supremely significant in the body-life of the local church. The over-emphasis on prophecy, healing and tongues needs correction not only in terms of more biblical definition but in giving an equal emphasis to those biblical spiritual gifts being neglected.

i. Families

Para-church ministries tend to be selective – young people, women, soldiers, nurses, students – and many such ministries started in attempts to reach special peer-groups. It cannot be over-stressed that the church is family-orientated, indeed Christian homes ought to be seen as the small groups into which churches sub-divide most naturally. Passages like Ephesians 5:21–22; 1 Timothy 3:4; Titus 1:6 need to be read in light of this. A local church needs the contribution brought by all the generations – grandparents, parents and children.

j. Universal membership

Para-church ministries are inevitably selective, and clearly a women's fellowship excludes non-women, just as any youth movement, by definition, excludes grand-fathers. A local church, however, is open to whoever wishes to come, irrespective of age, sex, race, colour, nationality, social class or intellectual ability (Gal. 3:28; Jas. 2:1–4). Those with differing views were not to be excluded (Rom. 14:1), nor even were unbelievers (1 Cor. 14:24–25). Thus though a Bible college may meet for 'services', in the very nature of the case, the service is restricted generally (though not absolutely, for nobody who wished to attend would be refused) to those studying and teaching and their families. It is clearly not a local church.

k. Missionary sending

This may seem a surprising inclusion in the marks of the local church (in spite of the author's known enthusi-asms!), and the more so as many para-church groups were raised up as 'missionary sending agencies'. How-ever, in recent years such societies have realized that it is more biblical to see the local church as the real sending agency (Acts 13:2; 16:2) and the para-church body as a specialist channel arranging organ transplants from the body of the sending church to the body of the receiving church. As we saw earlier in chapter 8, the local church is to be involved in evangelism not only in its own neighbourhood, but to the ends of the earth, and the sending function is thus an essential mark.

l. Giving for others

It is striking how much is said in the Acts of the apostles about giving. What is especially striking is that giving was within a local church (Acts 4:32–37), from one

185

church to another, from Antioch to Christians in Judea (Acts 11:29–30) and from European churches to poor 'Third World' churches, as the proud Greeks must have thought of Palestine, their former colony (Acts 24:27; 1 Cor. 16:1–3; 2 Cor. 8–9). Para-church movements are usually trying to persuade churches to give *them* money, except for those set up expressly for relief aid and so on. It is a mark of the local church that is does not spend its money in support only of its own members and activities, but of the universal church and of the poor and needy throughout the world.

Conclusion

Para-church activity, then, reminds us that although the church in its humanness is sometimes slow or reluctant to move, God is not limited to using only the churches as his instruments. He has always, even at the time of the early church (which was already conservative and reluctant to accept change, like accepting Gentiles!), been prepared to get some Christians to move unilaterally: Ananias (Acts 9:11–15); Peter (Acts 10) and the men of Cyprus and Cyrene (Acts 11:19–26). After a while, the churches come to recognize the hand of the Lord in such activity, and accept the rightness of what is being achieved. The para-church movements, then, serve the churches, and must be judged by the extent to which they do this: they are the 'free enterprise' of the churches.

Sometimes, though, the church has become so institutionalized, deformed or even apostate, that godly men and women feel they have no alternative but to revolt and rebel, and thus to go beyond 'renewal' to 'reformation' or what has been called 'restoration' of the church. Can it ever be right to do this, and is there any scriptural justification or biblical paradigms for such action? For while 'free enterprise' may be one thing, 'competition' is another.

chapter ten

THE RESTORATION
OF THE CHURCH
How radical may we be?

*As a prisoner for the Lord, then, I urge you to live a life
worthy of the calling you have received. Be completely humble
and gentle; be patient, bearing with one another in love. Make
every effort to keep the unity of the Spirit through the bond of
peace. There is one body and one Spirit — just as you were
called to one hope when you were called — one Lord, one faith,
one baptism; one God and Father of all, who is over all and
through all and in all.*

*But to each one of us grace has been given as Christ
apportioned it. This is why it says:*

> *'When he ascended on high,
> he led captives in his train
> and gave gifts to men.'*

*(What does 'he ascended' mean except that he also descended
to the lower, earthly regions? He who descended is the very one
who ascended higher than all the heavens, in order to fill the
whole universe.) It was he who gave some to be apostles, some
to be prophets, some to be evangelists, and some to be pastors
and teachers, to prepare God's people for works of service, so
that the body of Christ may be built up until we all reach unity
in the faith and in the knowledge of the Son of God and
become mature, attaining to the whole measure of the fulness
of Christ.*

Then we will no longer be infants, tossed back and forth by the waves, and blown here and there by every wind of teaching and by the cunning and craftiness of men in their deceitful scheming. Instead, speaking the truth in love, we will in all things grow up into him who is the Head, that is, Christ. From him the whole body, joined and held together by every supporting ligament, grows and builds itself up in love, as each part does its work. (Eph. 4:1–16)

Husbands, love your wives, just as Christ loved the church and gave himself up for her to make her holy, cleansing her by the washing with water through the word, and to present her to himself as a radiant church, without stain or wrinkle or any other blemish, but holy and blameless. In this same way, husbands ought to love their wives as their own bodies. He who loves his wife loves himself. After all, no-one ever hated his own body, but he feeds and cares for it, just as Christ does the church — for we are members of his body. 'For this reason a man will leave his father and mother and be united to his wife, and the two will become one flesh.' This is a profound mystery — but I am talking about Christ and the church. (Eph. 5:25–32)

What should we do if we are dissatisfied with the church that we belong to?

Well, first we should recognize that there would be something wrong with us if we were not occasionally dissatisfied with our church to a certain extent. After all, dissatisfaction is a product of the humanness of the church that we discussed in chapter 3.

Secondly, we need to recognize that it is not necessarily a lack of spirituality that causes us to be dissatisfied sometimes. The Old Testament prophets were extremely dissatisfied with the people of God, and, having been inspired by the Spirit, they criticized them very strongly. The apostles also were critical of the New Testament church, and if they had not been so we should not have most of the epistles that we read with such benefit today. The church is still imperfect, and the spiritual gift of discernment should not stifle our critical faculties but, if anything, should make us more sensitive to that which is displeasing to God both as individuals and as a church.

There are several courses of action open to us.

1. Faithful commitment to our congregation

Leaving a church is not something we should do lightly, but only after we have taken every possible step to see reformation and change.

1. We should pray for our local church and its leaders, as we pray for our own spiritual progress. To criticize the church and its leaders without talking first of all to the Lord of the church is folly. I have been very critical of local churches overseas, and needed to pray about my own attitude, as well as about those aspects which were disturbing me. It may be the very sameness and stereotyped monotony of the services, always singing the same hymns, or the same old choruses, or the poverty of the teaching with the same old hobby-horses trotted out week after week. It may be the absence of any purpose or progress in the church, the ineffectiveness of evangelism, the lack of warmth in the fellowship, or many other things. But we must identify ourselves with the sinfulness of the church and confess it.

2. We need to estimate objectively our own role in the church. If everyone else was as committed and active as we are, but no more so, would the church be better or worse than it is? If we criticize the failure of the church in evangelism, are we ourselves effective in winning others? If we criticize others for lack of prayer or lack of warmth towards one another, are we any better or are we part of the problem? It is arrogant pride, the 'we are holier than them' attitude, which is at fault.

189

3. After careful, prayerful consideration, we need to seek opportunity to share our difficulties with an elder, minister or other leader of the church (having been careful to avoid criticizing the leadership to others). This is clearly a difficult and sensitive step to take, and there are other, more tactful, alternatives to be attempted first. We can recommend or lend books we have found helpful, suggest a contact with a more effective model church, or contact with other church leaders at a conference. A minister in Pennsylvania told me that he had been converted after some years in the ministry through the faithful prayer and friendship of members of the congregation. If we remember the tactful way in which Priscilla and Aquila helped the gifted Apollos (Acts 18:26), we realize that it can be done.

4. We cannot assume that every other Christian must come to agree in all details with us! There is a devastating comment about J. N. Darby:

There was a frightening absence of any sign of willingness to stand with the other man, and con- sciously to understand why he thought as he did. Darby was characterised by all the arrogance of the man who has no doubt of his own rightness. The corollary to his sense of divine leading ... was that those who opposed him were the enemies of God: and he did not hesitate to say so ...[1]

It does not follow that because one disagrees with the pastor or the leaders of the local church, one is necessarily always right and they are wrong. I was much impressed when a young friend in a church with an insecure leader threatened by other gifted people in the church, commented that though he found the pastor difficult to get on with, and the teaching limited, the church itself was far more important, a far more precious thing than problems with the limitations of its leadership. If each congregation was no more than an aggregation of the particularly like-minded, and every strong-minded individual started a new congregation of his own, there would not be the kind of growth towards unity we discussed in chapter 4. Instead we would end up with what Muslims call a mosque of one and a half bricks.

Bishop Robert Daly said to Lady Powerscourt:

> You expect to meet with perfection, and you will be disappointed; it is not to be met with among any body of Christians in this sinful world. After a little time you will separate yourself from some who you will find not to be as perfect as you thought them to be; others will be added to the number; at last you will be left alone; and when you look into yourself, you will not find perfection there.[2]

5. We shall remember the importance the Scriptures themselves place upon unity (Eph. 4:1–5; Phil. 2:1–4) and the very strong warning against any who 'destroy the temple of God. God will destroy him' (1 Cor. 3:16). To run away from a difficult situation is the easy way. When the church in Corinth was split into different factions it never seemed to occur to the apostle that it would be straightforward for them to split off from one another in order to form separate congregations! If we speak of the church as the household or the family of God, splitting up the family is an unacceptable solution. Remember the discussion in chapters 2 and 3. The church is God's church: we cannot readily divide it or separate from it. It is also a human church, made up of sinful and fallible men and women. Even if we do separate from a church, we have no guarantee that the new church will be any better.

191

6. We shall learn from the experience of the past. We look back upon a whole series of attempted reformations of the church – the Protestant Reformation, the Methodist revival, the Christian Brethren attempt to restore New Testament Christianity, the Pentecostal revival and now the 'house churches'. The last represents a proper impatience with institutionalized Christianity, a genuine desire for a discipleship which produces changed lives. It is the most recent 'primitivist' movement attempting to restore the vitality of the early church, including healing, signs and wonders. (They embrace a Pentecostal interpretation which assumes that the Acts of the Apostles are *prescribing* what we should continue to do, rather than *describing* particular events of unique significance.)

The branch of the Brethren that developed into the 'Exclusives' sought to escape from the 'ruin of the church' and took the phrase 'to separate from iniquity' (1 Tim. 2:19) as shorthand for separation from the existing churches. They thus provide a useful paradigm for separatism. Anthony Norris Groves, a man of an entirely different spirit, responded:

> You ask me to give my opinion about separating from evil. I as fully admit as you can desire, that in my own person, it is my bounden duty to depart from every evil thing; but the judgement of others, and consequent separation from them, I am daily more satisfied is not of God.[3]

Groves explains this warm, non-separatist spirit as follows:

> If my Lord should say to me, in any congregation of the almost unnumbered sections of the Church, 'What dost thou here?' I would reply, 'Seeing Thou wert here to save and sanctify, I felt it safe to be with Thee.' If He again said, as

perhaps He may among most of us, 'Didst thou not see abominations here, an admixture of that which was unscriptural, and in some points error, at least in your judgement?' my answer would be, 'Yea, Lord, but I dared not call that place unholy where Thou wert present to bless nor by refusing communion in worship reject those as unholy whom Thou hadst by Thy saving power evidently sanctioned and set apart for Thine own ...' To the question, 'Are we not countenancing error by this plan?' our answer is ... so long as Christ ... walks in the midst of a congregation, blessing the ministrations to the conversion and edification of souls, we dare not denounce and formally withdraw from either, for fear of the awful sin of schism of sin against Christ and His mystical body.[4]

Only after we have exhausted every other possible kind of alternative over several years, does it seem to me that the possibility of leaving to form a new congregation should be considered. It would be better to find some other, more congenial, fellowship where the Scriptures are faithfully taught both to adults and children, where the Lord is adding converts from paganism (not some kind of separatist ghetto, a cave of Adullam [1 Sa. 22:2] where discontents from other churches gather!), and where true, spiritual warmth in fellowship and mutual encouragement are found.

Before we consider separation as a valid biblical option, we need to do some theological thinking about the character of God and his 'separation' from the failures of mankind and of the people of God.

The church in Ephesus was warned that unless it repented it could lose its lampstand (Rev. 2:5), and that was clearly possible, though it does not seem to have happened for another 1,300 years! It was possible for the Lord to withdraw his glory from his people (1 Sa. 4:22), just as Ezekiel later saw the glory of the Lord departing from the apostate temple in Jerusalem (Ezk. 10:18–19; 11:23). Has God withdrawn his glory from the Lutheran Landeskirche in Germany or from the Orthodox churches in Greece? We are very prone to write off other churches and dismiss them as apostate and dead. But has God?

At a conference of New Zealand Brethren discussing mission strategy over the next ten years, the subject of Korea came up. At that time there were no Brethren assemblies in that country, but there was a large number of very fine committed Christians and churches who had stood firm against fierce persecution from the Japanese and then from the Communists. Before starting a programme of assembly – planting, some prayerful thought had to be given to the status of believers in Korea – were they Christians or not? Were their churches churches or not, even if they did not meet as Brethren meet? We must avoid unthinkingly excommunicating those believers or churches which happen to have a different church order from our own!

So let us think about God and his attitude to sinful men and churches.

2. The character and work of God

If the church is so human, so frail and so sinful, how could it ever be beautiful? Are we not hopelessly idealistic and naïve to believe that this church has such a destiny? Has it not lost all its credibility? No. It will happen, because of the character of God, and because when he starts something he finishes it. My wife gives me little lists sometimes of unfinished jobs around the house: things I have started, but failed to finish. But that is because I am human. What God begins, he

194

finishes: '. . . being confident of this, that he who began a good work in you will carry it on to completion until the day of Jesus Christ' (Phil. 1:6).

a. The impartiality of God towards all people in Scripture as a whole

God has not given up on sinful mankind. Thus we are told that we should pray for 'all people' (1 Tim. 2:1, GNB). The logic of this command is then explained: there is only one God, who desires (not decrees) 'all people' to be saved and to come to a knowledge of the truth. There is only one mediator between people and God, the man Christ Jesus, who gave himself up as a ransom for 'all'. Because the Lord Jesus went to the cross to this end, and because it is the desire of God, we are to pray for every human being.

God is so impartial that he showers his blessings upon wicked and good equally generously (Mt. 5:45), and if we are his children we are to be equally generous and indiscriminate in loving others even if they are enemies who persecute us. This is what God is like: he gives the joys of home, marriage and children to all men and women whether they recognize him or not, call upon him or not, or are grateful or not. So Paul tells the people of Lystra that the God of creation is the one who 'fills your hearts with joy' (Acts 14:17).

Of course, I am not espousing universalism. Scripture also teaches that there are wheat and tares, sheep and goats, good fish and bad fish, those on the road to destruction as well as those on the road to life. But I am trying to remind you of the truth that our God is patient, faithful and gracious, and treats everyone alike even if they are wicked and unbelieving. And if God acts like this towards ungrateful unbelievers, how much more will he be gracious to those who profess to be Christians, even in churches which we regard as institutionalized and disobedient.

195

b. The faithfulness of God towards Israel in the Old Testament

What does the Old Testament teach us about the character of God?

If it teaches us one thing, it is surely that even if God's people, Israel, fail, God remains extraordinarily patient with them. Has the Lord written off the Jews who do not profess Jesus as Messiah and Lord?

> I ask then, Did God reject his people? By no means ... Again I ask, Did they stumble so as to fall beyond recovery? (Rom. 11;1, 11)

We are asking if there are limits to the grace of God. Where Israel is concerned, scriptural revelation itself tells us that the Jews will be grafted in again, that the return of the full complement (in modern Greek the word means 'crew') will be riches for the Gentiles, and their acceptance, life from the dead for the church.

> I the Lord do not change. So you, O descendants of Jacob are not destroyed. Ever since the time of your forefathers you have turned away from my decrees and have not kept them. Return to me, and I will return to you, says the Lord Almighty (Mal. 3:6).

Almost certainly he is echoing Lamentations 3:22:

> Because of the Lord's great love we are not consumed, for his compassions never fail, they are new every morning; great is your faithfulness.

Once again the argument is that if God is so faithful to the Jews, who make no profession of Christian faith, will he not also be faithful and not reject or give up on professing Christians in disobedient, compromising churches?

196

c. The patience of God towards the churches in the New Testament

When the Lord starts something, he does not give up or lose interest as if he were human. There is a tendency of some separatist 'house churches' to speak of older churches (*i.e.* all others), as 'old wineskins' and themselves as 'new wineskins'. These are biblical expressions and carry a quasi-biblical authority: but if we think about the character of God they are being used in an unbiblical way. To talk as if the rest of the churches are obsolete and can be left to rot impugns the character and faithfulness of God. It suggests that the Lord is interested only in novelties, in new splinter churches. It suggests that God loses interest in older churches, drops them, forgets them and leaves them on one side. But God is not like some petulant human child, with a short concentration span. He is faithful and lovingly persistent.

Even a doctrinally unsound, morally failing, divided church like Corinth is called 'the temple of God' (1 Cor. 3:16–17). No encouragement is given to split away even from a church as unsatisfactory as the one there. The passage is written in order to stop divisiveness.

The Lord's patience with the seven churches is remarkable. He certainly raises the possibility that he may 'remove their candlestick' (2:5) or spew them out of his mouth (3:16), but it is clear from these prophecies that he will not readily reject them, but goes on calling them to repentance. His gentleness is remarkable. He stands at the door, knocks and counsels. His feet are like burnished bronze. He could kick the door in, but he does not. His voice is like the sound of many waters, but he does not deafen them: he counsels.

It is not only what God is in his holy character, in his divine faithful being, but God's activity revealed in Scripture that should make us hesitate to rebel, revolt against and break away from his church.

d. The normal regular work of the Spirit in perfecting the church

Ephesians speaks in different ways of this regular work of God. Ephesians 2:21–22 speaks of our being built together into a holy temple through the work of the Holy Spirit. The prayer that concludes Ephesians 3 speaks of God's ability to do 'immeasurably more than all we ask or imagine', and is in the context of the goal 'to him be glory in the church'. Here is sufficient response to those whose pessimism about the church is such that they cannot 'imagine' a beautiful church. Ephesians 4 speaks of the gifts of humans; apostles, prophets, evangelists and pastors/teachers, which are used 'to prepare God's people for works of service, so that the body of Christ may be built up until we all reach unity in the faith . . .' (Eph. 4:12–13). Paul goes on to tell us:

> . . . Christ loved the church and gave himself up for her to make her holy, cleansing her by the washing with water through the word, and to present her to himself as a radiant church, without stain or wrinkle or any other blemish, but holy and blameless (Eph. 5:25–27).

That is a great and glorious statement of God's purpose, a purpose in which he is constantly engaged: in individuals, in congregations and in the universal church as a whole. But apart from the gradual and continuing work of the Spirit, there are also special times when he accelerates that growth and progress in the church.

e. The extraordinary work of the Holy Spirit in perfecting the church

There are times when everyone is talking about revival, and when there are nights of prayer for world revival and the like. There is no doubt that in the course of history the Lord has granted such 'times of refreshing' (Acts 3:19) as a result of repenting.

The Psalms contain such prayer for revival: 'Will you not revive us again, that your people may rejoice in you?' (Ps. 85:6). Psalm 80 has the repeated refrain, 'Restore us, O God' (verses 3, 7, 19) as well as, 'Return to us ...' (verse 14) and 'Revive us' (verse 18). Solomon's prayer of dedication of the temple again (2 Ch. 6) considers the possibility that the people of God may sin and need to repent, and pray for restoration.

The national revivals under Samuel (1 Sa. 7:2ff.), Josiah (2 Ki. 23) and Nehemiah and Ezra (Ne. 8) show that there were times of genuine repentance and turning to the Lord on the part of the whole people of God.

In the New Testament the time span is perhaps too short, but the call to five of the seven churches to repent corporately is an indication of the need for corporate repentance and revival. During the long subsequent history of the church, the Lord in his sovereignty has been pleased on many occasions to give revival frequently when and where it is least expected (*e.g.* East Thailand, Sarawak).

3. Reluctant withdrawal to start a new congregation

As has been indicated already withdrawal is a drastic procedure, only to be undertaken after long and prayerful consideration. It has to be a painful and retrograde step, because it is a reversal of the process by which the Lord is moving us forward to one perfected and glorified church in heaven (see chapter 4 on the unity of the church). We have failed 'to maintain the unity of the Spirit in the bond of peace', and we have retreated from 'the unity of the faith' instead of advancing towards it. There is an inconoclastic type of person who feels that a new start with himself at the head is bound to be better than anything that has gone before, and talks as though the Holy Spirit was unemployed in the church until his own arrival; but most of us are too humble to be that radical!

Usually such withdrawal is a desperate measure by frustrated Christians, and blame for the split may not lie so much with them as with the stubborn intransigence of those who have driven them out. They may have made long and sustained efforts to see their church renewed (using this word in a general sense rather than a specifically charismatic one) and reformed (that one too!). They have been made to feel that they are unwelcome or unspiritual, or they feel that their children are not getting properly taught from Scripture. Perhaps the real problem has been a personality conflict, but the two sides have polarized and have justified their differences by doctrinal criticism of each other. It may be frustrated impatience with the lack of vision or stick-in-the-mud nature of the local leadership. Especially in country districts there may well not be any viable local alternative congregation to which to transfer, and a new fellowship may be the only option.

If there is no real doctrinal difference of any significance, it may sometimes be possible for frustrated groups to agree to start some kind of outreach or daughter church from the parent, and thus turn a sad defeat into a victory. Just as new blackberry plants can be formed by 'layering' a branch to the ground until it takes root and forms a fresh plant, so the kind of church growth which can take place amicably, where all other attempts at reconciliation have failed, seems better than all the bitter works of the flesh (see the list in Gal. 5:19–21 including discord, dissensions and factions) that can result so often from disagreements.

Attempts are sometimes made to justify divisions as

the 'leading of the Spirit' ('the Lord told me' syndrome) and by arguing that that the new group is part
of God's plan to set up his 'kingdom'. The next chapter, therefore, seeks to clarify some of the very confusing ways in which people have used the concept of
'the kingdom of God'.

THE KINGDOM AND THE CHURCH
How do they relate?

'And I tell you that you are Peter, and on this rock I will build my church, and the gates of Hades will not overcome it. I will give you the keys of the kingdom of heaven; whatever you bind on earth will be bound in heaven, and whatever you loose on earth will be loosed in heaven.' (Mt. 16:18–19)

While they were eating, Jesus took bread, gave thanks and broke it, and gave it to his disciples, saying, 'Take it; this is my body.'
Then he took the cup, gave thanks and offered it to them, and they all drank from it. (Acts 14:22–23)

Everywhere one turns in the Church today the theme of the kingdom of God is being discussed . . . a rediscovery of the kingdom of God by widely different groups within the churches does not mean that everyone is agreed about its meaning and significance.[1]

Anyone attempting a biblical word-study of 'church' and 'kingdom' cannot but be struck by the fact that they hardly ever occur together in the same context: even finding both words in adjacent verses is rather difficult! It is as though they are entirely different categories in biblical thinking, as indeed in our conclusions we shall discover that they actually are!

None the less, there is a lot of confusion in many people's minds over the relation between 'church' and 'kingdom'. Some identify the two, some make the kingdom much wider than the church, and others now restrict 'kingdom churches' only to those churches enjoying a certain kind of discipline and pastoral authority. In view of this confusion we need to attempt to describe the variety of views and to define what the Bible teaches.

Respect for the authority of Scripture means using biblical words in a biblical way. Using biblical language out of its original context often negates and distorts its meaning. Merely using biblical words does not automatically authenticate the new meaning being given to a word. This situation is especially true today with the word 'kingdom', particularly when it is used as an adjective instead of a noun.

The use of biblical vocabulary somehow gives an appearance of quasi-authority, but it can be thoroughly *mis*leading if the biblical phrase is being *mis*appropriated. It has become fashionable to throw the word 'kingdom' around in a cavalier fashion: in theological works it is almost as popular as 'eschatological'. It is an 'OK word' in house–church circles: 'kingdom authority' and 'kingdom churches'. It is also a 'hurray word' which gives the correct politico-theological vibes among evangelical intellectuals! It gets very confusing when different Christian sub-cultures use the same words, derived from Scripture, yet with entirely different presuppositions and implications.

Varieties of usage of the word 'kingdom'

a. The Roman Catholic Church

Rome has established a political earthly kingdom, under an earthly human ruler, decked with pathetic earthly pomp, and at times in history seems to have identified the Roman Church with the kingdom of God. 'The Middle Ages are characterized by an often massive consciousness of a real kingdom of God present on earth.'[2] Hans Küng, himself a Roman Catholic theologian, in his extremely helpful book, *The Church*, indicates the progress of modern Catholic thinking about the church and the kingdom. In one particularly useful section[3] he says,

> It is impossible to speak of Christian society or even of the Church as being 'God's kingdom on earth', the 'present form of the kingdom of God', the 'forerunner of the kingdom of God'. But it would also be wrong to suggest ... that the Church builds up the kingdom of God, extends it throughout the earth, or works for its realisation. The Church, after all, prays not 'Let us realise Thy kingdom!' but 'Thy kingdom come!'[4]

We may have anxieties about the Pope's territorial ambitions when he kisses the airport tarmac on arrival in a country, but this is really little different from the Protestant missionary who climbs a mountain and claims what he sees for the Lord!

In considering Roman claims, we note that Matthew 16:18–19 is one of the few passages where the words 'church' and 'kingdom' are found in adjacent verses. Jesus speaks of building 'my community'. The existing use of *qahal* for the congregation of Israel suggests that Jesus means by this that Israel will be replaced by a new messianic community recognizing him as Messiah. It would seem gratuitous and anachronistic to read back the Roman or any other church into this declaration of Jesus. That new community will be built 'upon this rock' (*kepa*), an obvious word-play on Jesus' new name for Simon Bar-Jonah, Peter (*kepa*) in Aramaic, the language in which Jesus would have been speaking. The metaphor of the apostles as the foundation of the church is found again in Ephesians 2:20, and interpretation has only been confused by Roman Catholic claims and Protestant counter-apologetics.[5] Jesus then says that Peter will be given 'the keys of the kingdom of heaven', that is a delegation of God's sovereignty in binding (forbidding) and loosing (permitting). This 'loosing' authority he particularly fulfilled when he was God's instrument in admitting into the new Messianic community first Samaritans and then uncircumcized Gentiles (Acts 8:14–17; 10:1–11, 18; 15:7–11).

b. The Puritan hope that Jesus shall reign

This traditional evangelical expectation is frequently overlooked. Before the introduction of pessimistic, dispensationalist teaching that growing evil must dominate the world scene until the Lord's return, an entirely different spiritual optimism prevailed. Bible-believing Christians then awaited the universal spread and global triumph of the gospel, 'when the earth shall be filled with the knowledge of the Lord, as the waters cover the seas' (Is. 11:9). This is well expressed by the hymn:

> Jesus shall reign where'er the sun
> Doth his successive journeys run,
> His kingdom stretch from shore to shore . . .[6]

The Puritans, those involved in the great evangelical awakenings, and the founders of the modern Protestant missionary movement alike all looked forward to a time when 'through the work of the Holy Spirit in fulfilment of scripture promises, Christ would yet possess the earth'. A bright day would come when, in the words of Jonathan Edwards, 'the work of conversion will go on in a wonderful manner and spread more and more'.[7]

Andrew Fuller, friend of William Carey and first secretary of the Baptist Missionary Society, wrote:

If I should die, I shall be able to say to the rising generation, God will surely visit you. A work is begun that will not end till the world be subdued to the Saviour.[8]

To those of my own generation of young missionaries, 'seeking first the kingdom of God' meant giving one's life in commitment to planting churches overseas. In spite of all the other uses of 'kingdom' current today, it is as ambassadors of Christ, that we seek to extend his rule over human hearts.

c. The millennial reign of Christ on earth

Time does not allow a lengthy exposition of the view of Christ's millennial reign popularized in the Scofield Bible notes and still the dominant orthodoxy in the USA.

Donald Grey Barnhouse in his *Teaching the Word of Truth*[9] apparently intended for teaching children, provides a classic outline of the way this doctrine was taught in the USA. Lesson XIV, called 'Things to Come', explains the first coming when the Lord Jesus does not come all the way to earth but meets believers in the air: the rapture is compared to the action of a magnet picking up needles. The unsaved will be left on earth and will experience the great tribulation, during which time some will come to believe in the Lord in spite of fierce persecution. This will conclude with the battle of Armageddon and the return of the Lord Jesus down to earth to stand on the Mount of Olives.

Then He will set up His Kingdom here on earth ... the Lord Jesus will rule with a rod of iron ... Satan will not be free to tempt men then, for at the very beginning of the Kingdom he is bound and cast into the bottomless pit for a thousand years ... During the Kingdom, when anyone does wrong, it will be wholly his own fault, for he will

207

not be tempted by Satan ... the Lord will always
punish immediately ...[10]

Today most people would see the 'kingdom of heaven'
as Matthew's reverential way of describing the 'kingdom of God', in order to avoid direct use of the name
of God, a typically Jewish use appropriate to his
intended readership. It is not used in the other gospels.[11] The premillennial scheme differentiated the
two kingdoms, and did see the kingdom of God as the
inward and spiritual reign of God in the believer. However, the 'kingdom of heaven' according to this view, is
a kingdom on earth for one thousand years, a millen-
nium when Christ rules the world from Jerusalem, at a
time when all Jews will have become Christians and
rule with him. This means the postponement of the
kingdom of heaven into a future dispensation, and it is
a very literal kingdom geographically sited. By far the
worst thing about Darbyism was that expectation of
imminent return of the Lord (a good doctrine) led to
the unfortunate and wrongheaded conclusion that
such belief 'totally forbids all working for earthly
objects distant in time'.[12]

However, it did not stop them planting churches: J.
N. Darby himself was a remarkably successful and
indefatigable founder of congregations. (1,500
churches looked to him as founder or guide.)[13] The
American missionary movement, very much influenced by Dallas Seminary-training Bible college teachers
holds strongly to premillennial views, and it does not
seem to have been prevented from setting goals and
also planning for the future, or to have weakened
missionary resolve. In the US there has been a remarkable reversal of missionary theology!

The biblical usage of 'kingdom of God' is much
wider than as a term to describe a millennial kingdom.
There is a category confusion in using the word in a
territorial sense at all, compounded by making the

false distinction between Matthew's use of 'kingdom of heaven' and the 'kingdom of God' in the other gospels.

d. The kingdom of heaven established on earth – nineteenth-century liberalism

Walter Rauschenbush[14] argued that Jesus spoke a great deal about 'the kingdom' and only twice about the church, whereas Christ's followers became obsessed with the church and ignored the kingdom. To the 'Social-Gospellers' the 'kingdom of God' meant the establishment of a community of righteousness, every bit as much a saving act of God as individual conversion. The kingdom would be established through ethical teaching, social reform and political action.

Washington Gladden (1836–1918) anticipated that

> . . . every department of human life – the families, the schools, amusements, art, business, politics, industry, national policies, international relations – will be governed by the Christian law and controlled by Christian influences. When we are bidden to seek first the kingdom of God, we are bidden to set our hearts on this great consummation . . .[15]

> The kingdom of heaven is the entire social organism in its ideal perfection; the church is one of the organs – the most central and important of them all – having much the same relation to Christian society that the brain has to the body.[16]

Walter Rauschenbush (1861–1918) centred his theology on the kingdom of God, which he saw as a gradually evolving social order based on justice and righteousness. He emphasized biblical concern for the poor and oppressed, a concern which he found sorely lacking in the modern capitalistic system.

Competitive commerce exalts selfishness to the dignity of a moral principle. It pits men against one another in a gladiatorial game in which there is no mercy and in which ninety per cent of the combatants finally strew the arena.[17]

Rauschenbush wrote very powerfully about the nature of sin, a point which is picked up by Howard Marshall who comments:

Though we will reject both Ritschl and Rauschenbush because of their faulty theology of the kingdom ... Rauschenbush is right to emphasize that there is social sin as well as personal sin. It is also true that the causes of sin are to be found not merely in an inherited bias to sin within each individual but in a social and economic framework which tempted men to yield to that inherited bias.[18]

The Social Gospel movement motivated many sincere people, but it cut the nerve of evangelism, so that Edward Judson, son of the pioneer Adoniram Judson of Burma, declared, 'The important thing is not the building up of a church but the Christianisation of society.'[19] There was a fading of any real distinction between the church and the world. Those who accepted its basic assumptions found it difficult to conceive of a church that did not embrace humanity indiscriminately. The idea can be seen clearly in many hymns of the period. 'These things shall be: a loftier race than ere the world hath known shall rise ...', expecting to build Jerusalem in England's green and pleasant land! (In the same way, current views of the 'kingdom' are found in many of today's choruses and hymns.)

The Social Gospel was violently opposed by big business, which feared its socialism, allying itself with

American fundamentalism, which opposed the optimistic view of human society. The prophetic Bible conferences saw everything through the eyes of a pessimistic dispensationalism based upon biblical passages which depicted an ever-worsening state. The Social Gospel movement taught that the golden age, 'the kingdom of God' on earth, was right around the corner. D. L. Moody saw this as heresy: the world would get worse and worse until Christ came to establish his 'kingdom' on earth for a thousand years. American premillennial theology is pervasive and influential, seeing itself as the only orthodoxy. The unholy alliance between the theological and political right wing in the United States remains a problem for evangelicals elsewhere.

e. Identification of church and kingdom

Some evangelicals have assumed the identity of the church and the kingdom. Thus Geerhardus Vos writes:

> The church is a form which the kingdom assumes in result of the new stage upon which the Messiahship of Jesus enters with his death and resurrection. So far as the extent of membership is concerned, Jesus plainly leads us to identify the invisible church and the kingdom. It is impossible to be in one without being in the other. We have our Lord's explicit declaration in Jn. 3:3, 5 to the effect that nothing less than the new birth can enable man to see the kingdom or enter into it.[20]

As we shall see, to identify the kingdom with the church is to make a category error. The kingdom is not the same kind of thing as the church.

f. The restoration view of the kingdom

The restoration churches are the latest in a series of primitivist reform movements, wishing to restore the simplicity of the early church, and especially wanting to regard the apostolic age, rather than the present 'deformed' churches, as normative. Thus apostolic gifts, signs, wonders and healing are all to be restored. Authority structures, less obvious in Acts perhaps, are also seen as needing restoration. This pyramid structure of responsibility, sometimes called 'covering' or 'discipling' is seen as an expression of the kingdom of God.

> The essence of the kingdom of God was God's authority and the willingness of his people to let him exercise it over them ... God manifests his rule through 'delegated authorities' whom he appoints as his agents and through whom his authority is exercised ... How Christians relate to these authorities is crucial if they are to receive what Christ is giving through them and if they are truly to be in the kingdom of God. A kingdom person is one who has submitted his life to a delegated authority and similarly a kingdom church is one which submits to an apostle or a prophet ... To be truly in the kingdom everyone must submit to another who is over them in the Lord, who can call them to account and help them to mature ... churches are divided into 'kingdom churches' and the rest.[21]

Again, Andrew Walker writes:

> Salvation Army control is related to its hierarchical organisation which is self-consciously modelled on the secular army: orders are given at the top and passed down the line. In the Restoration churches, claims are made not only to belong to the Lord's army, but also to be subjects of the king in a theocratic state ... Firstly, against the conventional wisdom of denominational Christianity, it

insists that the charismatic gifts of the early Church have been restored and that God has re-established His control over the kingdom through a theocracy of apostles. Secondly, a belief in the restored theocracy has led to an ordering and control of believers' lives not typically found in conventional Christianity.[22]

Thus it is not merely a matter of giving free time to the church, but of giving one's all to the kingdom – time, money, possessions and skills. So 'kingdom life' is a total way of life, in a way that being a Baptist or a member of the Christian Brethren is not. However critical we may be of restoration theology as a whole, we must rejoice in this emphasis on full commitment as being a very good thing indeed.

What is so fascinating is that many of us sing about 'kingdom authority', without having consciously subscribed in any way to the underlying theology. (We can all sing 'Jesus is King and I will extol him . . .' because thus far it is biblical.) But authority in the restoration churches resides in a hierarchical organization seen as deriving from that king. There is, however, no evidence for this 'pyramid' structure of authority in the New Testament. Some wings of the restoration movement adduce Exodus 18:13–26 and Deuteronomy 1:9–18 as a basis for present-day church order. These passages tell how Moses divided the people of Israel, wandering in the wilderness, into thousands, hundreds, fifties and tens, each group responsible to its own leader. It does not seem proper to regard churches which do not accept this structure as being outside Christ's kingdom. That does seem a bit uncharitable!

The concept does, however, provide a useful way of persuading people to obey the teaching their leaders give them! The huge gap between what is taught in the pulpit and what is practised in the pews has baffled

Protestants who do not enjoy the constraints of the Roman confessional. The Wesley class-meeting was a partial solution. But now a way has been found of reducing this gap: a more efficient machinery for enforcing obedience now exists. But is it biblical?

Two passages seem especially relevant. In Romans 14:1–8 Paul is dealing with differences in observing days and food regulations, a problem between Christians of Jewish and Gentile origin in the congregations in metropolitan Rome. In spite of having apostolic authority (and having expressed his own views on such matters, *e.g.* in Col. 2:16; 1 Tim. 4:3–4), Paul insists, 'Each one should be fully convinced in his own mind.' Each individual Christian is finally answerable only to his own master, and *not* to any person, even if that person is an apostle!

In 1 Peter 5:3, Peter decrees that the leadership of elders is 'not lording it over those entrusted to you, but being examples to the flock'. This is an expression used by Jesus, and is clearly alluding back to Matthew 20:25 where Jesus contrasts secular Gentile oppressive leadership with the servant-slave ministry that he prescribes for his community.

Helpful and convenient though it may seem to be able to exact obedience and compel 'submission' from members of the congregation, it cannot be done, because the church is a 'voluntary' community. Christian individuals may choose to 'be subject', but they cannot 'be subjected' by others. Leadership is to be by example and service, not by domination!

g. Ecumenical universalism – middle twentieth century

Where confidence in the uniqueness of the Christian faith has been undermined, and where there is reluctance to describe any as being lost or perishing, where respect for the convictions of Muslims and Hindus leads to the danger of regarding their faith as equally

214

valid as the faith of Christians, a wishy-washy humanistic liberalism seems to speak almost as though everyone is saved or will be.

> God's Kingdom is domesticated on earth ... we have a return to Constantinianism and the idea of Christendom: the inhabited world is synonymous with the Kingdom of God ... It is – to say the least – naïve to hail all revolutionary movements as harbingers of the Kingdom.[23]

One of the most amusing examples of this was expounded by a speaker at the World Lutheran Federation, who spoke of the coming of the kingdom through Chairman Mao Tse-tung and drew parallels between the Long March and the Exodus.

We could see this Marxist-influenced liberalism as an updated version of the Social Gospel view, but we must hold the ecumenical movement and its theology responsible for the reversal of the remarkable church growth of Latourette's 'Great Century', the nineteenth. In the twentieth century, though the number of Christians has continued to increase as a product of an overall increase in world population, the percentage of Christians has decreased from 34% in 1900 to 32.5% in 1980. Ecumenical theology and crypto-universalism is a sclerosis that paralyses the nerve of mission, just as the Social Gospel did earlier.

h. Social evangelicalism – late twentieth century

The difficulty with this section is that it is a portmanteau from which a whole spectrum of views may be unpacked, many of them moderate and perfectly acceptable biblically in all but, perhaps, their attachment to the concept of kingdom!

Andrew Kirk expresses this helpfully when he questions how one was to,

215

... fit together all that the Bible has to say about social issues with its equally clear emphasis on the need for each individual to change his selfish way of life and receive from God forgiveness for wrong-doing and a new spirit. The answer that the Bible gives is the reality of the kingdom.[24]

The concept provides a convenient framework in which to fit both biblical and modern concerns, precisely because in Scripture it is such an elastic term, and it is possible to incorporate within it almost any emphasis which is not specifically 'church' and call it rather 'kingdom'.

Thus it is possible for those of us with politically socialist views to call ourselves 'Radical Christians' and to read our Bibles almost exclusively in terms of the struggle for a new kind of society – and some seem to use the word 'kingdom' as a kind of shorthand for this approach. They become so obsessed with the corporate, evil structures of capitalist society, that they lose sight of individual sin, forgetting that the poor are not only sinned against, but are themselves sinful. The cross is a symbol of the identification of a prophet with the oppressed, suffering at the hands of the rich and politically privileged.[25]

Other people hold views that are much more moderate, such as Christopher Sugden who writes:

The kingdom is God's programme of total redemption for every aspect of creation ...[26]

Howard Yoder[27] shows how in the synagogue sermon in Nazareth (Lk. 4.14ff.), Jesus read Isaiah 61:1–2a announcing the good news of the kingdom, 'in the most expressly social terms'. Yoder continues that Jesus announced a new regime offering liberation to the oppressed and blessing for the poor, what Yoder describes as:

216

a visible socio-political economic restructuring of relations among the people of God, achieved by his intervention in the person of Jesus as the one Anointed and endued with the Spirit.[28]

A report entitled *Evangelism and Social Responsibility* published in 1982 is much more cautious:

As the world lives alongside the Kingdom community, some of the values of the Kingdom spill over into society as a whole, so that its industry, commerce, legislation and institutions become to some degree imbued with kingdom values. So-called 'Kingdomised' or 'Christianised' society is not the Kingdom of God, but it owes a debt to the Kingdom which often is unrecognized.[29]

It can be seen that this 'overspill' model has its limitations, compared with the light, salt and yeast models used in Scripture:

So Jesus intends his followers neither to withdraw from the world in order to preserve their holiness, nor to lose their holiness by conforming to the world, but simultaneously to permeate the world and to retain their Kingdom distinctiveness.

We should notice that in many of these usages the word 'kingdom' has become a synonym for 'Christian', which can be substituted for it in most cases without any significant loss of meaning!

Howard Snyder has based a whole book on the relation between church and kingdom.[30] 'The church is God's agent for establishing his Kingdom . . . the Kingdom of God is the work of God; yet within God's plan there is room for man's action.'[31]

Those who follow 'creation ethics' base everything on norms laid down by God the Creator who has the right to order the lives of all people especially as laid down in the early chapters of Genesis. This means that ethics would remain the same whether or not Jesus came and taught. By contrast those who follow 'kingdom ethics' find their authority from teaching about the kingdom of God in the New Testament, especially the gospels. The lordship of Christ extends over all people, and not just believers. The 'powers' mentioned in Ephesians symbolize the evil structures of society which must be fought and opposed. It does not distinguish carefully enough between Christ's authority over unbelieving society, where his rights are still challenged by the usurper, and his acknowledged rule (kingdom) in the hearts of his redeemed community. The word 'kingdom' is applied to the world only in teaching about the return of Christ, when kingdom and world will become synonymous because all evil will have been purged out. Confusion arises because 'kingdom' is used both for his rule recognized within the church and for his rule and authority over all mankind, unrecognized by them.[32]

As David Bosch expresses it, with great clarity:

> The Church is that segment of the world which submits consciously to Christ, obeys and serves him albeit haltingly and with a stammer. The Church is not the world, for the Kingdom has already begun to manifest itself in her. And yet she is not the Kingdom, as the Kingdom is acknowledged and realized in her only partially and imperfectly.[33]

There is a considerable range of opinion between the extremes of more revolutionary liberation theology, and the moderate position of those who wish to take seriously the ethical teaching of Amos and Hosea and of the Lord Jesus for social justice and an end to oppression. We may feel that 'kingdom' is not the most biblically accurate way of stressing the importance of social justice, but we must be sympathetic to something that has plenty of other solid biblical foundations. I have always found Jacques Ellul's statement on this helpful:

> The Christian should participate in social and political efforts in order to have an influence in the world, not with hope of making a paradise, but simply to make it more tolerable. Not to diminish the opposition between this world and the kingdom of God, but simply to modify the opposition between the disorder of this world and the order of preservation that God wants it to have. Not to bring in the kingdom of God, but so that the gospel might be proclaimed, in order that all men might truly hear the Good News.[34]

The important question about all these different views and arbitrary annexation of the word 'kingdom' to a particular position is how far any of them are accurately reflecting the way that word is used in the New Testament itself. And it is to this question we now turn. Many of these views seem wide of the mark. We need Howard Marshall's biblical corrective:

> There is no programme of social action in the teaching of Jesus about the kingdom of God. He is concerned with the relationships of individuals to God and the behaviour that will result from that. On the one side, he offered the needy forgiveness, integration into the community of God's people, and physical healing. On the other side, he called those who followed him to a life in which their total attitude must be one of love to God and their neighbour and of commitment to himself as Teacher and Master.[35]

219

The biblical use of the word 'kingdom'

We have observed the confusion that has arisen because the translators of the New Testament chose the word 'church' when they would have been much better advised to have used the more people-centred word 'congregation'. In the same way, we should have been less confused if, instead of the word 'kingdom' (carrying with it the concept of territory and land), the translators had seen fit to use 'the reign' or 'the rule' of God.

The most helpful article on the biblical meaning of 'kingdom' is a short paper by my former colleague, Dick France, to which I am much indebted.[36]

He compares the question 'Is the church the kingdom of God?' to other meaningless questions like, ' Is an egg happiness?' or, 'Is Margaret Thatcher patriotism?' The church is a definable, empirical entity, but the kingdom of God is an entirely different category. It is not a material thing at all, a concrete kingdom, a territory or political unit, but the abstract fact that God reigns. It means 'the sovereign activity of God as ruler or king'.[37] The essential words are 'of God', so that 'the reign of God' is another way of speaking about the 'sovereign God'. Indeed, in Jewish literature 'the reign of God' is a reverential circumlocution for 'God'. 'The kingdom of God is near' means 'God is near'. It has its roots in the Old Testament understanding that God is king now and one day his kingship will be universally acknowledged among the nations.

The concept is central to the teaching of Jesus, who uses it sixty times (apart from parallels) in the Synoptic Gospels. It is an all-embracing word for the whole mission of Jesus, giving an overall conceptual framework: an umbrella word for all that Jesus came to achieve. As in the Old Testament it refers both to what is already true in the present (Mk. 1:15; Mt. 12:28;

Lk. 17:20–21) and something still awaited in the future (Mk. 9:1; Mt. 6:10; Lk. 19:11).

It often appears as an active verb: because God acts, God does things. It is a humanistic idea to suppose that people are able to bring about the kingdom through their efforts. It is a 'free gift' from God. That is important to remember: the kingdom is not 'achieved, or developed, or controlled or disposed of by men'.[38] It 'is near', it 'comes', 'appears', 'overtakes'; one is 'called' or 'invited' to it, or 'cast out' of it. God 'gives' it while people 'accept', 'take' or 'inherit' it. In that sense, those who receive it are the undeserving poor without qualification, the 'miserable' of the beatitudes. The sinners who had been excluded from Israel were now to be included in it. To repent was to accept the reign of God as a gift.

It is not so much a concept or an idea but a symbol whose function is to evoke a whole complex of ideas and emotions related to the belief that God is King. 'Thy kingdom come' and 'Thy will be done' are two ways of saying the same thing. Though 'kingdom' conveyed meaning to the Jews, Jesus extended its meaning. It meant salvation for Israel, but for more than Israel alone – the nations, a renewal of the world.[39]

Modern usage

The restricted use of the word 'kingdom' to mean social justice, or to emphasize that Christian concern extends beyond the spiritual, may be a very convenient short-hand, but it is misleading and dangerous. This is because there is a danger of importing this arbitrary and narrowed re-definition back into the New Testament, so that those sayings of Jesus[40] which refer to the kingdom of God are then assumed to be about social justice. Bibilical terminology re-defined by in-group usage can be very dangerous when imported back into the New Testament.

The purpose of the incarnation was emphatically not to introduce a human reform programme. Jewish hopes *were* political, but Jesus gave them no encouragement and 'systematically reinterpreted the nationalistic hopes of the Old Testament and later Jewish literature in terms of a spiritual liberation'. The danger of modern usage restricting it to a much narrower area than the New Testament does, is that it loses the richness of biblical meaning and runs the risk of distorting it. A perfectly correct emphasis is being expressed in inappropriate language.

'It is as wrong to *identify* the kingdom of God with social reform as it is to identify it with the church or with heaven.'[41] It is the same kind of category error.

Conclusion

We have spent some time seeking to understand biblical language in the context in which it first appears in Scripture, before trying to apply it to our own generation and culture. The fact that Scripture itself hardly ever brings the two categories together, and contains within itself no explanation or definition of their relationship, should make us very cautious about attempting to do what the apostles did not! Nearly all of the various uses outlined above use 'kingdom' in a different way from its biblical usage. They are not necessarily wrong in what they affirm – only in misusing a biblical phrase.

The house-church use of 'kingdom' as an adjective to describe what they do and what their congregations are in distinction to others is just another example of a misuse of a biblical word.

So the 'kingdom of God' means that God reigns. He already rules in heaven. And he rules in his church. Or does he? The restoration movement is right to ask the question. How far is he allowed to rule in our churches and how far are our activities determined by our tradition, rather than by what God has revealed in Scripture? It is possible to justify a great deal as being comformable with Scripture when you already do it, and not at all the same thing to derive something from Scripture from scratch.

In the Old Testament theocracy, God's people were often rebellious and refused to obey their king. The New Testament also gives us a picture of the church as being like a kindergarten full of squabbling and disobedient children. So I cannot end this chapter without asking myself how far I submit loyally to his rule in my own life – in my work, my home, my kitchen, my bedroom. We cannot leave the discussion of the kingdom as an intellectual novelty. How far do I allow him to rule as King in my own life, – for instance, in my attitudes to bereavement, illness and growing old? And how far do we as local congregations accept his rule, and submit to his sovereignty? It is not enough to sing that Jesus is King, unless we behave like loyal subjects utterly available in the service of his cause.

The church consists of people who acknowledge God as king and who are committed to proclaiming his kingship and witnessing to his reality in their own lives as individuals and as a community.[42]

THE DESTINY OF THE CHURCH

Does it have any future?

And we know that in all things God works for the good of those who love him, who have been called according to his purpose. For those God foreknew he also predestined to be conformed to the likeness of his Son, that he might be the firstborn among many brothers. And those he predestined, he also called; those he called, he also justified; those he justified, he also glorified.

What, then, shall we say in response to this? If God is for us, who can be against us? He who did not spare his own Son, but gave him up for us all – how will he not also, along with him, graciously give us all things? Who will bring any charge against those whom God has chosen? It is God who justifies. Who is he that condemns? Christ Jesus, who died – more than that, who was raised to life – is at the right hand of God and is also interceding for us. Who shall separate us from the love of Christ? Shall trouble or hardship or persecution or famine or nakedness or danger or sword? As it is written:

> 'For your sake we face death all day long;
>   we are considered as sheep to be slaughtered.'

No, in all these things we are more than conquerors through him who loved us.

For I am convinced that neither death nor life, neither angels nor demons, neither the present nor the future, nor any powers, neither height nor depth, nor anything else in all *creation, will be able to separate us from the love of God that is in Christ Jesus our Lord* (Rom. 8:28–39).

In post-Christian Europe it is possible to get depressed about whether the church has a future at all. Are we condemned to a shrinking clientele and increasing irrelevance? If we do not accept the pessimism of the premillennialists, what do we have to offer instead? Christians do not seem to think enough about the future of the church. Where is it going? If it is changing, is it for the better? What ought we to be working for? Do we expect to build the church of tomorrow simply by means of occasional bursts of Mission England-style evangelistic effort? ('What will we do when Billy Graham goes home?') Do we rely on periodical celebration events to cheer us up with triumphalist euphoria (whatever the downward trend of church statistics), while local churches stolidly maintain 'business as usual'? What can we expect?

The Bible tells us that two things will happen before the Lord Jesus returns in glory with his angels.

1. Two essential preliminaries to the end

The first of these is that 'this gospel of the kingdom will be preached in the whole world as a testimony to all nations and then the end will come' (Mt. 24:14). Paul speaks of the fullness (full complement) of Jews and all Israel being saved (Rom. 11:12, 28), and says that if the rejection of the Jews brought blessing to the other nations, their return will be like life from the dead (Rom. 11:15). And this goal of reaching every nation, every tribe, every 'people group' has been the thrust of evangelical missions over the past 200 years, even if some denominational groups have a diminished passion for saving souls and planting new churches. We are to expect continuing progress, and those of us who

226

have lived and worked in Africa, Asia and Latin America have seen it happening! The contrast with Europe is striking!

The second preliminary to the end is the perfecting of the church. We are to expect great progress. At present it is easy to be obsessed with the sins and failure of the church to fulfil biblical expectations. In preparation for the Lord's return, however, the church will become increasingly beautiful and credible: He will 'present her to himself as a radiant church, without stain or wrinkle or any other blemish, but holy and blameless' (Eph. 5:27). We think, talk and preach too little about this. Perhaps we feel it lacks credibility, and feel embarrassed and ashamed to hold up our heads in front of atheists, agnostics, scoffers and cynics and claim that the most significant thing happening in our human community is the church of Jesus Christ. Can they believe it? Do *we* believe it? We are to expect the churches to gain credibility, to be transformed more into Christ's likeness, and less conformed to the world. The Bible seems to teach that 'when he appears, we shall be like him' (1 Jn. 3:2). Unless we can envisage a chaotically divided church with its blots and wrinkles being instantly transformed, we are to expect a growing-up process into Christ, a steady renewal and reformation towards that perfect bride who will be fit and ready for the coming bridegroom.

If that change is to take place, then Christians need to have a much higher doctrine of the church and of what it is to become. So before we consider what will happen to individuals, the church and the whole universe when the Lord returns, we need to remind ourselves of the limitations of various views of the church.

1. The church is not merely an incidental 'means of grace' to help me as an individual to be saved. This is an individualistic view, which sees the church as there to help me. The church is regarded as a spiritual filling

station, where I can go for a weekly top-up of my spiritual tank.

2. Neither is the church a mere aggregation of Christians for worship and teaching. This is a more corporate view, but the church is still seen merely as a temporary association of believers for mutual help.

3. The church is more than an institutionalized gathering for breaking bread and preaching the gospel. This is the programme-centred view of the church.

4. And finally, the church is not merely a means to an end in the purposes of God but a significant end in itself.

Stated positively, the church is the people of God, established by him as a holy nation for his own possession. Initially it was almost exclusively Jewish, with a few proselytes and God-fearers from the Gentile nations. Following the exaltation of the risen Christ to glory, and the outpouring of his Spirit, it became a universal body. It soon had a majority of Gentiles and only a minority of Jewish believers. It has its origins in finite history, but its destiny lies in the infinite purpose of God.

Thus we insist that the church is *part of the gospel*, and it is also *part of salvation*. The church is God's destiny for mankind, for human individuals and for human society.

2. The church is the focus of God's purposes

a. The church is the Father's intended purpose – his family

'Simon has described to us how God at first showed his concern by taking from the Gentiles a people for himself' (Acts 15:14). The Scriptures as a whole, both Old and New Testaments, are about the purposes of God

228

to form a people for his own possession. He is not just intending to save a few individuals, but rather is concerned to bring into existence a new society, the new humanity, his own people. The Bible begins with one couple but finishes with a city. Humanity has always puzzled over the reasons for our existence, and in literature has dreamed about our destiny. The answers are to be found in the purpose of God in bringing the church into existence – human beings relating together in a new family, first of the local church, and then with other brothers and sisters in other local churches, and then . . . in the universal church, which will keep us all busy for eternity.

At the Lausanne Congress in 1974 there were two or three thousand people present. Because I had been privileged to travel rather widely in ministering to OMF home countries as well as the countries of East Asia, I realized that there were several hundred people present that I had met before and would like to spend time with. But with plenary sessions, seminars and other things to attend I began to realize that in a week I would be able to spend time with only a few people, let alone make new friends. There was time for the briefest of greetings, perhaps a handshake or a bow, or a distant casual wave for some. Perhaps a year might have been long enough to talk meaningfully with them all – perhaps not: say two-hour sessions, eight people a day (allowing for sleep). But eternity will give us chance to enjoy the whole worldwide Christian family. Some of us could do with spending more time with our own families unhurried by the next appointment or working day. How much more 'time' is needed if we are to get to know God's great international family.

The concept of the church as a family is part of the teaching of the New Testament. There are specific texts that call the church the household of faith (Gal. 6:10), the household of God (Eph. 2:19; 1 Tim. 3:15) or the family of God (1 Pet. 4:17). But there are a variety of other expressions that imply the same idea indirectly: brethren, and the love of the brethren (*philadelphia*) in particular. And a family points to a Father 'from whom his whole family in heaven and earth is named' (Eph. 3:15).

A chapter on this theme in *Cinderella with Amnesia* began with the individual human infant gradually becoming conscious of human faces beaming down fondly upon it, as well as human fingers poking its chin and ribs in order to assure themselves that the new arrival does respond to stimuli! Mother, father, siblings, relatives and friends are gradually identified in an ever-widening circle of human beings with whom the child must learn to relate.

People are social animals, and we are increasingly aware that a happy social environment is important for the healthy development of individual personality. The spoiled only child, 'little emperors' as they call them in China, are very different from those brought up in the hurly-burly of the large family. Still worse off are those who have been cruelly isolated for long periods on a desert island or in solitary confinement. A human infant raised in a laboratory, incubated, supplied with uncontaminated air and a balanced diet, would be physically healthy, yet, isolated from all human love and affection, would be socially maladjusted. Having heard no human voices, it would not develop language or the ability to communicate. It would not even know about smiling, laughing, holding hands, waving goodbye and so on. There would be no teaching, no discipline and only a little learning. The child would be retarded mentally and socially.

Experiments have been done on new born rhesus monkeys kept in isolation in a laboratory. After three months alone in a cage, such a monkey is introduced into a cage full of its normal, socially adjusted peers. The poor, artificially raised 'loner' can only cower in a corner and withdraws from all contact with other monkeys. It is socially maladjusted.

It is, however, alarming to find this 'rhesus syndrome' sometimes in ourselves, as 'trousered (or skirted) apes' entering a church building and looking desperately for an empty pew. Church buildings fill up from the back until each pew on both sides is occupied, and then someone has to make the frightening decision to sit down next to somebody else! Christians, born again of the Spirit, nourished through their own feeding on the Word of God, may yet be spiritually retarded defectives, congregationally maladjusted and finding it hard to relate to others. Encouragement, when singing certain choruses, to hold hands with strangers (or even to look into each other's eyes) produces in some of us remarkable symptoms of claustrophobia and a desire to escape by sinking through the floor. It is to be hoped that not all of us are that shy and self-conscious, but some of us can empathize with those who are! There is plenty of room for growth here, until we feel safe and at home in the family of God.

How can we help one another to relate better within the family of God? The congregationally retarded and socially maladjusted Christian needs to be persuaded that while in God's providence temperaments differ (we are not all supposed to be raving extroverts), isolated individualism is wrong and an excess of reserve may be cowardly and even pathological. When we are born again, we are born into the family of God and we need the support and stimulus of brothers and sisters in Christ. There is a proper Christian reserve and discretion, and it is wrong to force ourselves into others' privacy, or to lean on people to confess their innermost problems to all and sundry. But as the church develops towards its future destiny we expect to find a deepening relationship with the Father and with his family.

b. The church is the purpose of the Son's work – his body

'You shall call his name Jesus, because he will save his people from their sins' (Mt. 1:21). 'He loved the church and gave himself for it' (Eph. 5:25). The whole purpose of the finished work of Christ, and his continuing work within us, is to perfect the church.

When Jesus is talking about himself as the Good Shepherd of Israel, the Lord himself coming to shepherd his flock as foretold (Ezk. 34), he goes on to say: 'I have other sheep that are not of this sheep pen. I must bring them also. They too will listen to my voice, and there shall be one flock and one shepherd' (Jn. 10:16). Thus, though he sent the apostles only to the lost sheep of the house of Israel, he always has in view the bringing in of the Gentiles, and that is what Acts is about: all that Jesus 'continued to do' in the task of bringing those other sheep into the one flock. We spoke of the church as beginning with the small circle of the disciples in their personal attachment to their Lord and teacher. But just as we must expect to see a growing understanding of God as Father, so we need a growing consciousness of Christ-centred thinking in the church. I have recognized the danger of being such an enthusiast for the doctrine of the church that one can lose sight of the relationship of the body with the Lord Jesus as its head.

First, the Lord Jesus is *the source and growth point of the church*. 'We will in all things grow up into him, who is the head, that is Christ. From him the whole body ... grows' (Eph. 4:15). 'The Lord [that is the Lord Jesus] added to their number daily ...' (Acts 2:47). It is for this reason that people are said to be 'baptized into the name of the Lord Jesus'. Jesus is the Lord of the church: it is he who makes it grow.

Secondly, the Lord Jesus is *the unitive principle of the church*. Colossians 1:18 describes Jesus as 'the head of the body, the church', and these words significantly follow on from the statement that 'in him all things hold together'. He is so united with his church that Saul is told that when he was persecuting Christians, he was persecuting Jesus (Acts 9:5). Similarly the one who help 'one of the least of these brothers of mine . . . did it for me' (Mt. 25:40). He makes us members of his body (Eph. 5:30).

Thirdly, the Lord Jesus is *the focus of authority for the church*. 'God . . . appointed him to be head over everything for the church which is his body, the fullness of him who fills everything' (Eph. 1:22). Again there is 'one body . . . one Lord' (Eph. 4:4–5). The outstanding example of this is found in John's Patmos vision of the risen Lord speaking to each of the seven churches in turn. It is the Lord Jesus who walks between the seven golden lampstands holding the seven stars in his hand. His authority is overwhelming, his voice like the sound of many waters, yet he counsels them (Rev. 3:18); his feet are like burnished bronze, but he does not kick the door down – he knocks (Rev. 3:20). His authority is plain, but he speaks to us, in order that we may exercise our own wills in loving obedience to him.

Fourthly, the Lord Jesus *sacrifices in order to save his church*. 'Christ loved the church and gave himself for it' (Eph. 5:25). His leadership is seen in his sacrificial giving, and this becomes a model for the husband who takes the initiative in giving and sacrifice out of love for his wife.

As the church, the bride, moves towards the royal wedding, there will be increasing love for the Lord Jesus and dependence on him. He has given us his Holy Spirit as a pledge (2 Cor. 1:22; 5:5; Eph. 1:14), a word sometimes used in the ancient world for an engagement ring. As we approach closer to that great anticipated royal wedding, we shall expect to find an increasing Christ-centredness in all our thinking.

c. The Holy Spirit's purpose is perfecting the church — his temple

'And in him you too are being built together to become a dwelling in which God lives by his Spirit' (Eph. 2:22). The present work of the Holy Spirit in giving both gifts and graces is with a view to building the church. While Scripture does speak of the individual (1 Cor. 6:19–20) as indwelt by the Spirit, it also speaks of the Holy Spirit 'among' the corporate people of God (1 Cor. 3:16; 2 Cor. 6:16). 'Be filled with the Spirit. Speak to one another with psalms, hymns and spiritual songs. Sing and make music in your heart to the Lord, always giving thanks to God the Father for everything . . . . Submit to one another out of reverence for Christ' (Eph. 5:18–21). These verses refer not to an individual experience of the Spirit, but to a congregational experience in worship. Ephesians 2:21 speaks of the church as 'a holy temple in the Lord' reminding us that the purpose of the *Holy* Spirit is to make his temple *holy* also.

It is surprising, in view of the renewal emphasis on the ministry of the Holy Spirit, that there are relatively few new hymns and choruses that focus upon the work of the Holy Spirit. We need a fresh concern for the holiness of the whole church as we move towards the 'end'. Our theology must have room for some greatly overlooked biblical ideas expressed in words one does not often hear Christians use, or at any rate not in the sense in which they are used in Scripture. These two words are translated in the NIV as 'restoration' and 'renewal'! But in Scripture they are talking not about what God is doing in the present, but about what God will do in the future. Peter speaks of this when he says Acts 3:21, 'He must remain in heaven until the time comes for God to restore everything, as he promised long ago through his holy prophets.' So apostles and prophets tell us of this great anticipated 'restoration' of all things.

But we have an even greater witness to this future destiny: the Lord Jesus himself uses a second striking word when he says, 'I tell you the truth, at the *renewal* of all things, when the Son of Man sits on his glorious throne, you who have followed me will also sit on twelve thrones, judging the twelve tribes of Israel' (Mt. 19:28). The word 'renewal' was used by the Stoics for that restoration of nature every spring, when everything is bursting with new life. Yet what appears in the spring is not totally discontinuous with what precedes it, but the anticipated fulfilment of it. The 'renewal of all things' will make our children's picture-book illustrations of the garden of Eden look like a rubbish dump or a wilderness by comparison.

The Bible then contains significant teaching about the future destiny of human individuals, of the church and of the whole universe.

3. The three levels or dimensions of salvation

a. Individual

'The Lord Jesus Christ ... will transform our lowly bodies so that they will be like his *glorious* body' (Phil. 3:21). In the Apostles' Creed Christians down the centuries have declared their faith in 'the resurrection of the body'. It is true that as evangelicals we have tended to preach a gospel to individuals, and talked of 'personal salvation' and of Jesus as a 'personal Saviour'. We have rightly insisted that each individual needs to repent and believe for himself, by personal appropriation of the merits and benefits of Christ's death and resurrection. This is good and proper.

But, in doing so, we have sometimes given the impression that 'salvation' is chiefly individual, about an individual's standing with God, and all the posthumous benefits which stem from this. There will be not only resurrection but transformation into his likeness.

Salvation must include this 'individual' aspect, and any gospel which leaves it out is no gospel at all. However, to preach this alone reduces the scope of the gospel in a way that is not true to Scripture. Our critics would say that our concerns were selfish and revolving mainly round our own personal survival after death.

Before we look into this criticism further, however, the point should be noted that, while the human body does decay, it will be resurrected and remoulded.

b. Corporate

'Christ loved the church and gave himself up for her to make her holy ... and to present her to himself as a *glorious* church, without stain, or wrinkle, or any other blemish (Eph. 5:27).

Just as we are encouraged to know that our failing human bodies will be replaced by new ones, so we are vastly encouraged when we realize that the churches, with all their familiar spots and blemishes, will become a perfect human society. How frequently our young people are discouraged and disillusioned by their churches. But just as our mortal, imperfect, human bodies are decaying, so also our corporate congregational bodies are full of imperfections. This concept of the future perfection of the church is clear in the intensive verb used of perfecting the church: 'he who began a good work in you will carry it on to completion until the day of Jesus Christ' (Phil. 1:6). So we anticipate not just saved individuals, but a perfected human society in glory. The writer to the Hebrews makes constant future reference to the destiny of God's people: 'the city with foundations, whose architect and builder is God' (Phil. 11:10), 'we are looking for the city that is to come' (Heb. 13:14), and 'they were longing for a better country – a heavenly one' (Heb. 11:16).

I have lived in several countries, and Singapore was in many ways the best, but in all of them their citizens had their complaints and longings for something better still. Patriotism and love of our own countries still leaves us all dissatisfied and with an unfulfilled longing for a perfect human society. This dissatisfaction is reflected in literature like *Utopia* or Priestley's *They Came to a City*, and in more modern science fiction and fantasy writing.

Future salvation, then, is not just saved individuals and redeemed lone rangers, but a glorified church – a perfected human society as described in Revelation 21 – 22, using the language of the bride and the holy city. Our expectation of heaven must include this corporate concept.

To summarize: while the church may be imperfect now, she will be transformed into Christ's heavenly bride, purified, beautiful, radiant in love for him, sharing his glory.

c. Cosmic

'The creation itself will be liberated from its bondage to decay and brought into the *glorious* freedom of the children of God' (Rom. 8:21, see context). It is not only individuals and the church who will enter into final salvation, but the whole of God's created universe. Just as our human aspirations for a perfected human society will be fulfilled in Christ, so also will our appreciation of the natural world be fulfilled, as we walk on holiday, or lie on our backs watching fluffy clouds scud across a blue sky and feel the coolness of the grass on our faces.

Too often evangelical Christianity has treated the souls of men as brands plucked from the burning and the world in general as a grim vale of soul-making. It has been content to see the splendour of the created universe, together with all the brilliant achievements of human labour, skill and thought, as nothing more than the expendable backdrop for the drama of redemption. One of

237

the reasons why men of our generation have turned against conventional Christianity is that they think it involves writing off the solid joys of this present life for the doubtful acquisition of some less substantial treasure.[1]

It is here that Genesis 1 and Revelation 22 come together, as is so beautifully described in Romans 8. Everything created by God is good. According to Revelation 21:24–25 even human achievements will not be lost: 'the kings of the earth will bring their splendour into it ... the glory and honour of the nations will be brought into it.' If even human achievements will have their place in the heavenly Jerusalem, how much more will the glories of God's creation. In turn this gives to us a positive theological place for human culture, music and art, as well as for those studies and hobbies that focus upon what God has made.

The whole magnificent theatre of the universe, together with all its splendid properties and all the varied chorus of sub-human life, created for God's glory, is cheated of its true fulfilment so long as man, the chief actor in the great drama of God's praise, fails to contribute his rational part. The Jungfrau and the Matterhorn and the planet Venus and all living things too, man excepted, do indeed glorify God in their own ways; but since their praise is destined to be not a collection of independent offerings but part of a magnificent whole, the united praise of the whole creation, they are prevented being fully that which they were created to be, so long as man's part is missing, just as all the other players in a concerto would be frustrated of their purpose if the soloist were to fail to play his part.[2]

238

The late Donald M. MacKay used to speak of an 'ejector seat theology', the notion that when the human body is beginning to break up like a destructing aircraft, the human soul ejects from it like a parachuting pilot. This is a Greek idea more than a biblical one. However, some Christians have often embraced a similar idea in relation to the world in which we live. The church in rapture is seen to be ejected out of a world rushing to destruction, like some kind of celestial Dunkirk.

But when God created the world, he 'saw all that he had made, and it was very good' (Gn. 1:31). Even after the Fall, Scripture speaks of the physical universe in a very positive way: 'The earth is the Lord's and everything in it' (Ps. 24:1) and 'the whole earth is full of his glory' (Is. 6:3). The Lord Jesus said, 'Blessed are the meek, for they will inherit the earth' (Mt. 5:5). Above all Romans 8 seems to suggest that the whole creation is waiting for the glorious liberty of the sons of God rather than for total destruction. But there are passages about the heavens wearing out like a garment and being rolled up like a robe (Heb. 1:11–12), or the destruction of the heavens by fire (2 Pet. 3:12). How do we reconcile these? Well, just as the human body is destroyed, but resurrected and remoulded; just as the church is full of faults and blemishes, but will one day be transferred; so also the heavens and the earth will be remade as the new heavens and the new earth. If we know that all God created is good, we have a quite inadequate doctrine if we imagine it will all be destroyed as totally expendable. Certainly Revelation 21:24, 26 suggest that only what is evil will be destroyed and that all that is good will be brought into the holy city to be enjoyed.[3]

Conclusion

Our concept of God, of salvation and of human destiny in Christ has been too small, too narrow, too constricted. We have so often failed to realize and to proclaim a full gospel of salvation that includes the individual, the social and cosmic dimensions of God's great purposes. We need prophetic poets and writers like C. S. Lewis to stir our imaginations through works such as the Narnia Chronicles or *Voyage to Venus*.

Now why say all this? Because we need for a moment to take our eyes away from the human problems of our little local congregations, and look to the glories of what lies ahead. In many churches we are pessimistic about the present, seeing it as only the prelude to tribulation and final cataclysmic disaster. But there are these other teachings in Scripture which can be so easily overlooked by those brought up in a Darbyist scheme of premillennial dispensationalism. The church so often does not attract because its view of the 'end time' justifies poor evangelism, presenting salvation as a way of escape from this wicked world. We are sometimes in danger of despising our inheritance and rejecting the world, for which Christ died to reconcile all things to himself, and in which the common grace of God falls on just and unjust alike. Sometimes we seem to have abandoned a world, which God himself has not abandoned.

If we have the biblical doctrine of the future destiny of the church in our hearts, instead of being pessimistic we shall be characterized by the neck-craning expectancy of Romans 8:19. This view of the destiny of human beings, of human society in the church and of the whole universe, is one that makes sense and provides the answers to the deepest human longings and aspirations. It is God himself who through his Spirit has put into our hearts these longings 'that words cannot express' (Rom. 8:26). And the God who is able to do exceeding abundantly above all that we ask or imagine will more than fulfil both our prayers and our imagination.

Our responsibility

One of A. A. Milne's stories is built around Christopher Robin and Pooh dropping twigs over one side of a bridge into the stream below, and then rushing across the bridge to watch them float through on the other side. Many Christians seem content to float limply along like 'Poohsticks' in the current of God's purposes, instead of facing responsibilities and swimming, like fish, purposefully within the stream.

> Continue to work out your salvation with fear and trembling, for it is God who works in you to will and to act according to his good purpoose (Phil. 2:12–13).

These verses express our responsibility perfectly. In the context 'your salvation' seems to apply not to the gaining of eternal life, but to the solving of the corporate problems of the congregation in Philippi, where Christians are not 'like-minded' or 'one in spirit and purpose' (2:2). Instead the church is being hindered by selfish ambition, vain conceit (verse 3) and self-centred concern for individual interests (verse 4). Christians are to accept responsibility and so 'work out' their own solution. At the same time, they are to recognize that they are in the stream of God's purposes, for through his Spirit he is at work in them. They are not to abdicate from 'willing' and 'doing', but as they do so they are enabled to overcome that weakness of purpose endemic to sinful humanity, and even more, that inborn inability to do what they intend. There are hymns which suggest that the will may be handed over

241

once for all so that 'it shall be no longer mine', but this is never suggested in Scripture. God is not glorified by programming us for unwilling obedience, but by our repeated choosing to obey, when we might have disobeyed. In this instance, obedience calls us to enthusiastic effort participating in the churches' progress towards future perfection, which God intends to bring to fulfilment.

The biblical expectations of a perfected church, without spot or wrinkle (Eph. 5:27), having arrived at 'the unity in the faith' (Eph. 4:13), will be fulfilled. Sometimes one fears that this will be in spite of us, for we seem so half-hearted in our desire for a glorious church. So many seem content to float along within the flow of God's purpose, without so much as a quiver of fins or tremor of tail. Just as the Philippians were commanded to obey, submitting to the lordship of Christ, by 'working out' salvation for their local church, so we too must all work within our local churches for their growth into wholeness, and indeed concerned for the universal church and its perfecting. We have the sure knowledge of God's revealed destiny for the church, and the certainty that he will work in us to will and to do of his good pleasure.

POSTSCRIPT
Why should I belong to a local church?

If you have persevered to this point you should not be in any doubt at all that the church is part of the gospel and part of salvation. Being a disciple of Jesus must mean not only that you have a personal attachment to him, as your Saviour and Lord, but that you are committed to those who share that discipleship with you, and who are equally committed to his cause.

There are two or three pathological options to be avoided.

1. There is the mistaken view that one does not need 'the church', which is usually seen as a building to be attended, an institutional 'cultus' to be observed, rituals and ceremonies to be observed. As this book has tried to make clear, those represent mistaken and anti-scriptural views of what the church is.

2. There is the view that we can worship God on our own – which is true, except that one would wish to modify it to say, we *must* worship God on our own, but that we *must* also meet and worship with others, and benefit from our mutual interaction. 'Fellowship' is the jargon word! Certainly we can, and we should, both pray and read the Scriptures on our own, but our own resources are limited and we can be helped by the shared understanding of the Scriptures that others have, and especially of those who are gifted by God to

teach and explain the Scriptures to others, and who will have had opportunity for special training to improve their study and teaching skills. That is, we need the church to teach us, to build us up, to deepen our own understanding of the Bible. Our enthusiasm for God and our personal prayer life will probably vary with health, appetite and even the weather(!), and our ups and downs need the help and stimulus of our fellow-disciples.

3. There is the mistaken view that we can float around as spiritual freelances, benefiting from many different congregations without being committed or attached to any. Instead of being a member (not in a club membership sense) of a body, intimately related to other members, we are more like lice, ticks or fleas that live as parasites on church bodies. If we hear of a warmer church body elsewhere we can always hop across and enjoy a good spiritual suck there as well! This kind of parasitic spiritual 'lone ranger' sees the benefit of attending one or more congregations, without being committed to any. He or she fails to make a contribution through service either verbally or non-verbally and is like a grumbling appendix of no apparent positive use to the body, a clot in the blood-stream . . . This kind of person fails to see that we need more than teaching from the church, and more than an opportunity to share in singing and listening. We need the kind of positive input, rebuke and admonishing that can come only when someone is willing to be known as an individual in long-term commitment to a group. The floating non-member is ignoring discipline, and is failing to recognize the significance of the social, corporate aspect of salvation, and God's purpose in calling us into a community.

In contradistinction to these wrong attitudes, there is the person who sees that he or she needs a local church, and that a local church needs him or her. We need more than a preacher and teacher; we need overseers, we need friends and spiritual brothers and sisters. Discipleship has to be worked out in community, in fellowship with others, who contribute to our growth as we contribute to theirs. You cannot fly solo to heaven, with a little formation flying on Sundays. Each one of us needs a closer involvement with fellow-disciples, an interlocking relationship like the members of a body, who sustain, stimulate and strengthen each other.

May I then urge you, reader, if this book has been of help to you, but you have not up till now belonged to any local congregation of Christians, to determine before your Teacher and Lord to find and join such a group without delay, and to dedicate your energies henceforth to seeking to perfect and beautify that congregation until it is a credible and consistent community of the new humanity in Christ.

NOTES

Chapter 1

[1]Michael Griffiths. *The Example of Jesus* (Hodder and Stoughton, 1985)

[2]John Taylor, *The Primal Vision* (SCM, 1963), p. 18

[3]I. Howard Marshall, *How Far Did the Early Christians Worship God?* (*Churchman*, vol. 99, no. 3, 1985), p. 224

[4]The word derives from the verb 'to call' (*kaleō*), actually the radical *klēsia*, its passive form, together with the prefix *ek*, meaning 'from' or 'out of', so that the group is not an accidental aggregation of people but is made up of those whom God has specifically called out and summoned together.

[5]I. Howard Marshall, *op. cit.*, p. 224

[6]Emil Brunner, *The Misunderstanding of the Church* (English translation, Lutterworth Press, 1952), p. 12

[7]Lesslie Newbigin, *The Household of God* (SCM, 1953), p. 25

[8]F. W. Beare, *The First Epistle of Peter* (Black, 1958), p. 101

[9]Frank E. Gaebelein (ed), *The Expositor's Bible Commentary*, vol. 9, *Acts* (Pickering and Inglis, 1977), p. 446

[10]*New Bible Dictionary* (IVP, [2]1982), p. 229

[11]Alan Stibbs, *The Church, Universal and Local* (Church Book Room Press, 1948), p. 69

[12]Alan Stibbs, *God's Church* (IVF, 1959), p. 66

[13]K. L. Schmidt, quoted in G. Kittel, *A Theological Dictionary of the New Testament*, vol. 3 (Eerdmans: Grand Rapids, 1968), p. 503

[14]Hans Küng, *The Church* (Search Press, 1968), p. 263

247

[15]David Michell in *Japan Harvest Magazine* (date unknown)
[16]Theodore Roszak, *The Making of a Counter Culture* (Faber and Faber, 1968), p. 150

Chapter 2
[1]This suggestion, which immediately occurred to me on seeing them, is also given a scholarly mention in Andrew E. Hill's article, *The Temple of Aesclepius: An Alternative Source for Paul's Body Theology?* in *Journal for Biblical Literature* (1980).
[2]Paul S. Minear, *Images of the Church in the New Testament* (Lutterworth Press, 1960), pp. 18ff.
[3]*Ibid.*, p. 23
[4]Robert Brow, *The Church: An Organic Pattern of its Life and Mission* (Eerdmans: Grand Rapids, 1968)
[5]See Cranmer, *The Lord's Supper* (London, 1907), p. 101
[6]For a helpful treatment of this issue see Alan Cole, *The Body of Christ* (Hodder and Stoughton, 1964)
[7]Lesslie Newbigin, *The Household of God* (SCM, 1953), pp. 28–29

Chapter 3
[1]Lesslie Newbigin, *The Household of God* (SCM, 1953), p. 81
[2]Hans Küng, *The Church* (Search Press, 1968), pp. 319ff.
[3]Article xix of the Thirty-nine Articles of the Church of England
[4]Hans Küng, *op. cit.*, p. 263

Chapter 4
[1]Paul S. Minear, *Images of the Church in the New Testament* (Lutterworth Press, 1960)

Chapter 5
[1]Gavin Reid (ed.), *Hope for the Church of England* (Kingsway, 1986)
[2]Canon John Poulton, *Fresh Air* (Marshall, Morgan and Scott, 1985), p. 111
[3]See Stephen Smalley, *Conversion in the New Testament*, in *Churchman* (September 1964), pp. 200ff.
[4]See *A Man's Life* (Church Pastoral Aid Workbook, 1986)
[5]*Ten Sending Churches* (MARC Europe, 1985). p. 30

Chapter 6
[1]Terry Virgo in *New Frontiers* (June 1987)
[2]Emil Brunner, *The Misunderstanding of the Church* (Lutterworth Press, 1952), p. 60

[3]I. Howard Marshall, *How Far Did the Early Christians Worship God?* (*Churchman*, vol. 99, no. 3, 1985)

[4]Robert Banks, *Paul's Idea of Community: The Early House Churches in Their Historical Setting* (Paternoster Press, 1980), p. 91

[5]*Ibid.*, p. 92

[6]I. Howard Marshall, *op. cit.*, p. 220

[7]Emil Brunner, *op. cit.*, p. 60

[8]*Ibid.*, p. 61

[9]I. Howard Marshall, *op. cit.*, p. 224

[10]*Ibid.*, p. 224

[11]*Ibid.*, p. 227 (italics added)

Chapter 7

[1]Donald English, *'Tell It As It Is': Some Reflections on Communicating the Gospel Today* (Laing Lecture, 1983, published in *Vox Evangelica* 14, 1984), p. 9

[2]*UK Christian Handbook 1987–88* (MARC Europe/Evangelical Alliance/Bible Society)

[3]Jo Bayley, *The Gospel Blimp* (Cook, 1960)

[4]J. Grayston (ed.), *Care to Say Something?* (Mission England/SU, 1982)

[5]*A Man's Life* (Church Pastoral Aid Society Workbook, 1986)

[6]Michael Wooderson, *Good News Down the Street* (Grove Books, 1982)

[7]John Chapman, *Know and Tell the Gospel* (Hodder and Stoughton, 1981)

[8]*Ten Sending Churches* (MARC Europe, 1985)

[9]From *Mission Fingers of God* (MARC Europe, 1985)

[10]William Carey, *An enquiry into the obligation of Christians to use means for the conversion of the heathens* (Leicester, 1972), p. 13

Chapter 8

[1]*UK Christian Handbook 1987–88* (MARC Europe/Evangelical Alliance/Bible Society), p. 11

[2]Alan Stibbs, *Christian Ministry* (Falcon, 1960), p. 10

[3]J. N. D. Kelly, *The Pastroral Epistles* (Black, 1963), p. 107

[4]See, for example, Martin Thornton, *Spiritual Direction* (SPCK, 1984)

[5]See Nigel Wright, *The Radical Kingdom* (Kingsway, 1986), pp. 101ff.

[6]J. D. M. Derrett, *'Where Two or Three are Convened in My Name . . .': A Sad Misunderstanding* (*Expository Times*, vol. 91, December 1979)

[7]Michael Griffiths, *Serving Grace: Gifts Without Inverted Commas* (MARC Europe, 1986)

[8]Ray Schulz, *Romans 16:7: Junia or Junias?* (*Expository Times*, 1987), pp. 108–110

[9]C. E. B. Cranfield, *International Critical Commentary*, vol. 2 (T. & T. Clark, 1979), p. 788

[10]Dr Catherine Kroeger has suggested that the Gnostic distortions of the Adam and Eve story lie behind 1 Timothy 2. For example, it was said that Genesis 3:20, 'mother of all that live', meant what it said and that she was the mother of Adam too (Hippolytus, *Refutations*, v. 16. 9ff.): 'when Adam . . . opened his eyes . . . he said, "You will be called 'the mother of all the living' because you are the one who gave me life"' (*On the Origin of the World*, 115:31 – 116:17, NHL 172), and again, 'When he saw her he said, "It is you who have given me life; you will be called 'Mother of the Living' – for it is she who is my mother"' (*Reality of the Archons* (11:4) 89. 11–16). The Apocryphon of John speaks of Adam being deceived.

If these were the 'Jewish myths' in circulation in Ephesus, Paul's words which insist that Adam was created first and Eve deceived make sense.

Chapter 9

[1]*UK Christian Handbook 1987–88* (MARC Europe/Evangelical Alliance/Bible Society), p. 8

[2]Ralph Winter, *Churches needs missions because modalities need sodalities* (*Evangelical Missions Quarterly*, Summer 1971), p. 195

[3]J. R. W. Stott, *Co-operating in World Evangelization – A Handbook on Church/Para-church Relationships* (Lausanne Occasional Papers, no. 24), p. 13

[4]H. Evan Hopkins, *Charles Simeon of Cambridge* (Hodder and Stoughton, 1977), p. 151

[5]*Ibid.*, p. 121

[6]See F. F. Bruce, *New Testament History* (Pickering and Inglis, 1982), pp. 65ff.

[7]*Theologisches Worterbuch zum Neuen Testament*, ed. G. Kittel and G. Friedrich (Stuttgart, 1932–74), III:503. English translation, *Theological Dictionary of the New Testament*, ed. G. W. Bromiley, 10 vols. (Grand Rapids, 1964–76).

[8]J. B. Lightfoot, *The Epistle to the Colossians* (Macmillan, 1880), p. 176

[9]Emil Brunner, *The Misunderstanding of the Church* (Lutterworth Press, 1952), pp. 64ff.

[10]*Ibid.*, p. 60

[11]*Ibid.*, p. 61. The subject has an extensive literature. See especially J. R. W. Stott, *Baptism and Fullness* (IVP, 1975) and Michael Griffiths, *Serving Grace: Gifts Without Inverted Commas* (MARC Europe, 1986)

Chapter 10

[1]F. R. Coad, *A History of the Brethren Movement* (Paternoster Press, 1968), p. 111

[2]Mrs Hamilton Madden, *Memoir of the Rev. Robert Daly*, quoted by F. R. Coad *op. cit.*, p. 207

[3]F. R. Coad, *op. cit.*, p. 122

[4]*Ibid.*, p. 116

Chapter 11

[1]Andrew Kirk, *A New World Coming* (Marshall, Morgan and Scott, 1983), p. 41

[2]Hans Küng, *The Church* (Search Press, 1976), p. 91

[3]*Ibid.*, pp. 88–104

[4]*Ibid.*, p. 92

[5]See R. T. France, *Matthew* (Tyndale Commentary, IVP, 1985), pp. 254–256

[6]Isaac Watts' paraphrase of Psalm 72, published as early as 1719

[7]Ian Murray, *The Puritan Hope* (Banner of Truth, 1971), p. 150

[8]Ryland, *Life of Andrew Fuller* (1816), p. 536

[9]Donald Grey Barnhouse, *Teaching the Word of Truth* (Eerdmans: Grand Rapids, 1940)

[10]*Ibid.*, p. 132

[11]See R. T. France, *op. cit.*, p. 46

[12]F. W. Newman, quoted by W. B. Neatby in *A History of the Plymouth Brethren* (Hodder and Stoughton, 1902)

[13]F. R. Coad, *A History of the Brethren Movement* (Paternoster Press, 1968), p. 106

[14]Walter Rauschenbush, *A Theology for the Social Gospel* (1919)

[15]Washington Gladden, *The Church and the Kingdom* (New York, 1984) in *The Social Gospel in America*, ed. Handy (Oxford University Press, New York, 1966), p. 105

[16]*Ibid.*, p. 105

[17]Walter Rauschenbush, *History of Religion in the United States* (Prentice Hall, 1960), p. 492

[18]Howard Marshall, *The Social Implications of Christ's Teaching and Ministry* (*Christian Graduate*, September 1964), p. 4

[19]Winthrop Hudson, *American Protestantism* (University of Chicago Press, 1961), p. 142

[20]Geerhardus Vos, *The Kingdom of God and the Church* (Presbyterian and Reformed, 1972), pp. 85–86

[21]Nigel Wright, *The Radical Kingdom* (Kingsway, 1986), pp. 83–84

[22]Andrew Walker, *Restoring the Kingdom* (Hodder and Stoughton, 1985), p. 120

[23]David Bosch, *Witness to the World* (Marshall, Morgan and Scott, 1980), p. 216

[24]Andrew Kirk, *op. cit.*, p. 46

[25]*Ibid.*, p. 21

[26]Christopher Sugden, *Radical Discipleship* Marshall, Morgan and Scott, 1981), p. 23

[27]Howard Yoder, *The Politics of Jesus* (Eerdmans: Grand Rapids, 1972)

[28]*Ibid.*, pp. 35–39

[29]*Evangelism and Social Responsibility* (Grand Rapids Report, Lausanne Committee, 1982), p. 34

[30]Howard Snyder, *The Community of the King* (IVP, USA, 1977)

[31]*Ibid.*, p. 13

[32]M. Schluter and R. Clements, *Jubilee Institutional Norms: A Middle Way Between Creation Ethics and Kingdom Ethics as the Basis of Christian Political Action*

[33]David Bosch, *op. cit.*, p. 222

[34]Quoted by Carl Henry in *Aspects of Social Ethics* (Eerdmans: Grand Rapids, 1964), p. 96

[35]From Howard Marshall, *The Hope of a New Age: the Kingdom of God in the New Testament* (Themelios, vol. II, No. 1, September 1985)

[36]Dick France, *The Church and the Kingdom of God – Some Hermeneutical Issues in Biblical Interpretation and the Church: Text and Context*, ed. D. A. Carson (Paternoster Press, 1984), p. 30

[37]Howard Marshall, *op. cit.*, p. 5

[38]Ben F. Meyer, *The Aims of Jesus* (SCM, 1979), p. 131

[39]*Ibid.*, p. 135

[40]*Ibid.*, p. 40

[41]*Ibid.*, p. 41

[42]Howard Marshall, *op. cit.*, p. 14

Chapter 12

[1]G. C. B. Caird, *The Christological Basis of Christian Hope*, in *The Christian Hope* (SPCK, 1970)

[2]C. E. B. Cranfield, *Some Observations on Romans 8:19–21* (in *Reconciliation and Hope*, edited by R. Banks [Leon Morris Festschrift, Exeter, 1974], p. 227)

[3]Please forgive me if this eschatology is different from yours! We study an infallible word, but we do not have infallible expositors. 'We know in part and we prophesy in part' (1 Cor. 13:19) and 'we see in a glass darkly' (1 Cor. 8:2). So please have sympathy and patience with your brother as he seeks to understand and explain the Scriptures.

Take my life

MICHAEL GRIFFITHS

It's an all-or-nothing, round-the-clock commitment. Following Jesus means unconditional obedience, sacrificial service, and total devotion to God's will.

Michael Griffiths shows us what the Bible says about serving the Lord with all our will, time and money; all our mind and love; all that we do or say, and all that we are.

190 pages   Pocketbook

Inter-Varsity Press

The Cost of Commitment
JOHN WHITE

'For years I felt guilty because I never seemed to be committed deeply enough to Christ... I had the feeling that I should be suffering more, doing without more. Yet when I did suffer, my suffering bore little relationship to my commitment. Sometimes it seemed to arise from my lack of commitment and at other times bore no relation at all to it...

'When Jesus tells you to take up your cross daily, he is not telling you to find some way to suffering daily. He is simply giving forewarning of what happens to the person who follows him.'

A warm and personal book to help Christians count the cost of commitment.

"...message is presented in a lucid, readable, at times very moving style.."   Evangelical Times

".. useful book to place into the hands of those who have recently made the great decision."
Christian Herald

91 pages   Pocketbook

Inter-Varsity Press